MW01602232

KURDISTAN

History, Regional Relations, and the Road to Sovereignty

Divina West

KEY Publishing
PO BOX 162
Jenks, OK 74037

For information, address KEY Publishing
Rights Department, PO BOX 162, Jenks, OK 74037.

For information about special discounts for bulk purchases, please contact KEY Publishing.

Manufactured in the United States of America

10 9 8 7 6 5 4 3 2 1

Library of Congress Cataloging-in-Publication Data is available.

ISBN 978-1-63732-857-6 (Print Book)
ISBN 978-1-63732-858-3 (ebook)

CONTENTS

ABSTRACT

The Kurds are an ethnic group, indigenous to the Mesopotamian plains and the highlands in what are now southeastern Turkey, southwestern Armenia, northeastern Syria, northern Iraq, and northwestern Iran. The Kurds are often referred to as the world's largest ethnic group without a state. They have experienced violent repression by authoritarian rulers throughout the 20th century, developing fervent nationalism and catalyzing militant movements to defend Kurdish rights and attempt to win self-rule and independence. Using secondary data analysis and archival study, this paper seeks to answer the question, 'what are the roadblocks to Kurdish sovereignty?' in a historical context to holistically analyze their current situation in the region. Qualitative complying of history and research revealed that over a century of war and suppression furthered the Kurdish diaspora and though Kurds have achieved autonomy in Iraq, they still face external and internal roadblocks to sovereignty. Further research revealed that internal issues perhaps pose more of a roadblock than external ones, specifically, economic and political instability and division being the most problematic.

INTRODUCTION

The Kurds are the world's biggest ethnic group without a state. They have been subject to violent repression but have resiliently sought independence. After the fall of the Ottoman Empire, they were left without a state and their population split between four newly drawn states and borders. The Kurds most recently rose to fame for the role they played in the war against the Islamic State. The Kurds were one of the United States' strongest allies in the war but were then abandoned when the US removed troops from Syria. However, the Kurds are no stranger to betrayal and proxy wars.

The Middle East has a complicated history full of regional conflicts. We have to understand the context and history of the region in order to better understand current events and create sustainable policies and thus sustainable peace. This now more important than ever with the failed referendum. Recent events have highlighted that though Kurds are nearly unanimous in their desire for a Kurdish state, they are not as close nor ready for independence as we once thought, and state building is not a simple task.

This book will cover over a century of complicated history with a focus on the breakup of the Ottoman Empire, suppression from surrounding regimes, international and civil wars, the establishment of the Kurdistan Regional Government in Iraq, and the fight against the Islamic State. Within the context of that history, this paper then covers the most current status of the Kurd's at the forefront of the war against the Islamic State and their regional relationships with Turkey, Syria, Iran, and Iraq. Within the context of their complicated history, this paper then evaluates the internal and external factors on the Kurd's road to sovereignty.

CHAPTER 1

History

There is a saying among Kurds: "No friends but the mountains." This refers to the oppressing state governments and dictators surrounding the region. The mountains are very important to Kurds. They have not only shaped the history, people, tradition and culture, they have also been used more practically as hideouts for Kurdish Peshmerga's and guerrillas fighting oppressive regimes ("Land & Environment" n.d.). This saying highlights their ties to the land and the mountains, but also how they have a long history of being betrayed and left to fend for themselves. The Middle East has a complicated history full of intricate conflicts. To understand current events and create sustainable policies, a person has to understand the context and history of the region. In this chapter, I cover over one hundred years of history in chronological order to highlight the complicated and multifaced nature of the history of the Kurds. This chapter covers key points in Kurdish history including: language, ancient history, post-Ottoman Empire, the First Gulf War, the establishment of the autonomous region of Iraq, and the war against the Islamic State. This chapter highlights the themes of internal and external conflict, suppression, and betrayal. The purpose of this chapter is to build historical context on which the rest of the paper builds.

Background

The Kurds are an ethnic group and are one of the indigenous people of the Mesopotamian plains and the highlands in what are now southeastern Turkey, southwestern Armenia, northeastern Syria, northern Iraq, and northwestern Iran (BBC News 2019). They speak Kurdish, an Indo-European language, with several dialects. The Kurds are a diverse yet distinctive people and community. The majority of Kurds are Sunni Muslim, but a number of Kurds practice a variety of religions and creeds (BBC News 2019). The Kurds are the region's fourth-largest 3 ethnic group ("The Time of the Kurds" 2017). They are also known as the world's largest stateless people group. It is estimated that between 25 and 35 million Kurds inhabit the extensive plateau and mountainous area known as Kurdistan (BBC News 2019). The Kurdistan ("Land of the Kurds") designation refers to an area of Kurdish settlement that roughly includes the mountain systems of the Zagros and the eastern extension of the Taurus.

Language and Culture

The Kurdish people are a diverse people. The Kurds are a heterogeneous ethnic group whose ethnic background comes from many regions including Iraqi Kurdistan, and parts of Iran, Turkey, and Syria. The Kurdish ethnic group includes many ancient ethnicities that have been absorbed into modern cultures including Iranian, Azerbaijani, Turkic and Arabic cultures. In this sense, the Kurdish culture shares commonalities with many other regional cultures. Kurdish culture celebrates diversity and exhibits tolerance ("Learn About Kurdish Culture" n.d.). The Kurds are not mono-lithic, however, and tribal identities and political interests often supersede a unifying national allegiance. Some Kurds, particularly those who have migrated to urban centers, such as Istanbul, Damascus, and Tehran, have integrated and assimilated, while many who remain in their ancestral lands maintain a strong sense of a distinctly Kurdish identity ("The Time of the Kurds" 2017). The development of their culture and language has been heavily affected by historic repression from surrounding states, their lack of a homeland and auton-omy and their diaspora. This has resulted in diversity but also a lack of cohesion between the various groups.

The Kurds speak a language related to Farsi ("Factbox: The Kurdish Struggle for Rights and Land" 2019). Kurdish dialects are broken into three main groups: Northern Kurdish, Central Kurdish and Southern Kurdish. Northern Kurdish dialects, Kurmanji, are the most common. 4 However, Turkey banned anyone from speaking Kurmanji Kurdish from the 1920's until 1991. It was even illegal to speak the word "Kurd." Therefore, there are less resources for learning Kurmanji Kurdish (which is more popular in Turkey) than the other Kurdish languages. The Sorani dialect in Central Kurdish is spoken by less than one fourth of all Kurds. Sorani is the dialect with the most well-developed literary tradition in modern times because an educational system in Sorani Kurdish was allowed to develop in Iraq. In the autonomous region of Iraq, the Kurdistan Regional Government, recognizes Kurmani and Sorani, and promotes both dialects being taught in schools ("Learn About Kurdish Language" n.d.).

Historically, The Kurds have experienced years of cultural repression. In Turkey, Iran, Iraq and Syria, there were extensive campaigns at forced assimilation. Kurds were forbidden to speak Kurdish in public and they had to change their names to local ethnic names if they wanted a job or to enroll their children in school. Their books, music and clothing were considered contraband and they had to hide them in their homes. If authorities searched their homes and found anything Kurdish, they could be imprisoned, and many were. In recent years, both Iran and Turkey have relaxed their systemic cultural repression, and Iraqi Kurds have achieved autonomy ("Learn About Kurdish Culture" n.d.). Often referred to as the world's biggest ethnic group without a state, the traditionally nomadic Kurds have been subject to violent repression by authoritarian rulers throughout their history and into the 20th century. This has catalyzed nationalist and militant movements to defend Kurdish rights, language, and culture and win self-rule (Pitel and Cornish 2019).

Pre-Ottoman Empire

Since ancient times, the area we now know as Kurdistan has been the home of the Kurds, a people whose ethnic origins are uncertain ("Kurdistan | History, Religion, & Facts" n.d.). 5 Despite the Kurdish people's long history in the land, they have never had permanent land nor achieved a nation state (BBC News 2019). However, the extensive plateau and mountainous area which covers large parts of eastern Turkey, northern Iraq, northwestern Iran and smaller parts of northern Syria and Armenia, is commonly referred to as Kurdistan.

It roughly includes Zagros and eastern Taurus mountain ranges. For 600 years after the Arab conquest and their conversion to Islam, the Kurds played a recognizable part in the troubled history of western Asia. However, they operated as tribes, individuals, or turbulent groups rather than as a distinctive people with their own land. Among the Kurdish dynasties that arose during this period the most important were the Shaddādids, ruling a predominantly Armenian population in the Ānī and Ganja districts of Transcaucasia (the Marwānids of Diyarbakir (990–1096); the Ḥasanwayhids of the Kermānshāh region (c. 961–1015); and the ʿAnnazids (c. 990/91–1117), who initially ruled from Ḥulwān. Less is written of the Kurds under the Mongols and Turkmen, but they again became prominent in the wars between the Ottoman Empire and the Ṣafavid dynasty. Several Kurdish principalities developed and survived into the first half of the 19th century, notably those of Bohtān, Hakari, Bahdinan, Soran, and Baban in Turkey and of Mukri and Ardalan in Persia. But Kurdistan, though it played a considerable part in the history of western Asia, never enjoyed political unity ("Kurdistan | History, Religion, & Facts" n.d.). Furthermore, after World War One and the end of the Ottoman Empire, the victorious Western allies laid out a plan to create a Kurdish state in the 1920 Treaty of Sevres. But the pledge made by Britain, France and the US to the Kurds went unfulfilled as the allies were unable to secure borders (Danforth 2015).

Treaty of Sèvres

One hundred years ago, European powers carved up the remnants of the Ottoman Empire. In Paris, the Treaty of Sèvres was planned and signed in 1920 only to quickly fall apart. 6 That treaty barely lasted a year, but the world is still being affected by it today. The Treaty of Sèvres internationalized Istanbul and the Bosphorus, while giving pieces of Anatolian territory to the Greeks, Kurds, Armenians, French, British, and Italians. Seeing how and why the first European plan for dividing up the Middle East failed, we can better understand the region's present-day borders, as well as the contradictions of contemporary Kurdish nationalism and the political challenges facing modern Turkey (Danforth 2015).

The 1916 Sykes-Picot agreement divided the Middle East into British and French zones of influence and delineated the borders of the modern Middle East. Following World War I, the Treaty of Sèvres, signed in 1920, dissolves the Ottoman Empire and in the drawing up of new borders, proposes and included the creation of an autonomous Kurdish state. Unfortunately, within a year of signing the Treaty of Sèvres, European powers realized they were hasty in signing the treaty and did not have the level of control nor upper hand they had presumed. Determined to resist foreign occupation, Ottoman officers like Mustafa Kemal Ataturk, Turkey's new leader, rejects Sèvres and reorganized the remnants of the Ottoman army. After several years of desperate fighting, they successfully drove out the foreign armies seeking to enforce the treaty's terms. Thus, the Treaty of Lausanne, replaced the Treaty of Sèvres merely three years after the signing of Sèvres. The result was Turkey as we recognize it today, whose new borders were officially established in the 1923 Treaty of Lausanne. The Treaty of Lausanne, negotiated with the new Turkish government, omitted any reference to a Kurdish homeland, and the Kurds were left stateless. Kurdistan was never created because it was not drawn up in the Treaty of Lausanne as it was in the Treaty of Sèvres. The Kurds, inhabiting previously Ottoman territories, were dispersed across the newly demarcated borders of Turkey, Iraq, Syria, and Iran, and repeatedly revolt against the respective authorities. The failure of the Treaty of Sèvres left 7 the Kurds with minority status in their respective countries. Over the next century, any move made by the Kurds to create independent state has been brutally quashed (BBC News 2019) (Danforth 2015) ("Factbox: The Kurdish Struggle for Rights and Land" 2019) ("The Time of the Kurds" 2017) (Pitel and Cornish 2019).

The Treaty of Sèvres has been largely forgotten in the West, but it has a potent legacy in Turkey, where it has helped fuel a form of nationalist paranoia some scholars have called the "Sèvres syndrome" (Danforth 2015). Sèvres certainly plays a role in Turkey's sensitivity over Kurdish separatism, as well as the belief that the Armenian genocide—widely used by European diplomats to justify their plans for Anatolia in 1920—was always an anti-Turkish conspiracy rather than a matter of historical truth. Moreover, Turkey's foundational struggle with colonial occupation left its mark in a persistent form of anti-imperial nationalism, directed first against Britain, during the Cold War against Russia, and now, quite frequently, against the United States. Yet to the Kurds, The Treaty of Sèvres was the rightful treaty and their lost promise of a homeland. The false hope and failure of the Treaty of Sevres was the beginning of a complicated history of Kurdish nationalist groups entering into alliances with powerful nationstates only to then be abandoned when those countries' short-term interests have been fulfilled (MacDonald 2019). As the Ottoman Empire came to an end, their hope for a state dashed, Kurdish Nationalism began (Danforth 2015) ("Factbox: The Kurdish Struggle for Rights and Land" 2019).

Post-breakup of the Ottoman Empire

The Kurd's quest for a homeland began in the early 20th century. With the dissolution of the Ottoman Empire after World War I and particularly with the encouragement of U.S. Pres. Woodrow Wilson—one of whose Fourteen Points stipulated that the non-Turkish nationalities of 8 the Ottoman Empire should be "assured of an absolute unmolested opportunity of autonomous development"—Kurdish nationalists looked to the eventual establishment of a Kurdistani state. ("Kurdistan | History, Religion, & Facts" n.d.). Many Kurds began to contemplate the establishment of a homeland—usually referred to as "Kurdistan." That hope and fight are alive today, after one hundred years of conflict.

In 1923 a Turkish-centric, centralized state faced uprisings from Kurdish tribes. In reaction to these uprisings, policies repressing Kurdish rights and identity were put in place. Kurdish languages were banned and Kurds were forced to "Turkify" their names, as well as the names of towns and villages (Pitel and Cornish 2019). Sheikh Mahmud Barzanji rebelled against British rule and declared a Kurdish independent kingdom in northern Iraq. In July of 1924, the British defeat Barzanji and the short-lived kingdom of Kurdistan fell (BBC News 2017). The League of Nations decides Mosul will be part of Iraq in 1925 with a provision for rights for Kurds ("History | Unbelievable Kurdistan—Official Tourism Site of Kurdistan" n.d.). In 1932, uprisings in the region of Barzan, Iraq/Kurdistan arose in protest of Iraq's admittance to the League of Nations and in demand for Kurdish autonomy. These demands were ignored. Mullah Mustafa Barzani led another uprising in 1943 and won control of large areas of Irbil and Badinan. In August of 1946, British Royal Air Force bombing forced Kurdish rebels over the Iraq-Iran border, fleeing into Iran, where they joined Qazi Mohamed and Iranian Kurds. Qazi Mohamed founded an independent Kurdish state in Mahabad.

The Republic of Mahabad and the KDP—Iran

On January 22, 1946, Kurds establish the Republic of Mahabad. Mustafa Barzani founded The Kurdistan Democratic Party (KDP) and the KDP held its first congress in Mahabad. Mustafa Barzani is considered the father of Kurdish nationalism and was the founder of the KDP 9 in 1946, while in exile in the Republic of Mahabad. Originally named the Kurdish Democratic Party of Iraq and then renamed the Kurdistan Democratic Party, it was the only Kurdish party in Iraq until the 1970s. The KDP remains the dominant Kurdish party ("The Time of the Kurds" 2017). The Republic of Mahabad, was a short-lived, independently governed state in Kurdinhabited territories of Iran that then came under Soviet control during World War II. The Soviet Union, occupied Iran alongside the Allies and tried to annex the country's north-west, encouraging Kurdish nationalism and the establishment the Republic of Mahabad. The short-lived republic was destroyed when the Soviets pull out. Iran then reoccupied Mahabad after the Soviet withdrawal in December 1946. The "Mahabad Republic" collapsed under attack from Iranian forces, and Mustafa Barzani fled to the Soviet Union (BBC News 2017) (Pitel and Cornish 2019) ("The Time of the Kurds" 2017).

A Revival of Kurdish Nationalism—Iraqi Kurds Rebel

In 1951 a new generation of Kurdish nationalists revived the KDP. Mullah Mustafa Barzani was nominated president though he remained in exile in the Soviet Union. Thus, the real leader of the KDP was Ibrahim Ahmad, who favored close ties with the Iraqi Communist Party. In 1958, the Iraqi monarchy was overthrown which allowed Kurdish nationalists to organize openly after years in hiding. A new Iraqi constitution was then created which recognized Kurdish "national rights" and Mullah Mustafa Barzani returned from exile. Later in 1958, on returning to his homeland of northern Iraq, Mustafa Barzani, led an uprising for an autonomous Kurdish nation. This started a war against the Iraqi state that lasted until 1970. In 1960, relation between Kurdish groups and the Iraqi government became strained. The KDP claims repression is increasing (BBC News 2017). The KDP is dissolved by the Iraqi government in 1961after Kurdish rebellion in northern Iraq. The Iraqi government of Abdul Karim Qasim refused Mulla 10 Mustafa Barzani's request for Kurdish autonomy (BBC News 2017) ("History | Unbelievable Kurdistan—Official Tourism Site of Kurdistan" n.d.) (Pitel and Cornish 2019). In reaction to unfulfilled promises of autonomy under the rule of Abd al-Karim Qasim, Mustafa Barzani launched a Kurdish rebellion in 1961. On September 11th, Mustafa Barzani issued a proclamation to all Kurds, calling them to take up arms against the forces of the Iraqi government and thus, the Kurdish revolution started.

Fighting continued throughout the decade against multiple Iraqi regimes. In 1968, Iraq's Baath party, a regional branch of the pan-Arabist socialist movement, came into power. In March of 1970, the Baathist government detailed plans for Kurdish autonomy. Iraqi government and the

Kurdish parties agreed a peace accord, which granted the Kurds autonomy. The accord recognized Kurdish as an official language and amended the constitution to state that: "the Iraqi people is made up of two nationalities, the Arab nationality and the Kurdish nationality" (BBC News 2017). The Kurdistan Democratic Party (KDP), lead by Mulla Mustafa Barzani, reaches an agreement with Baghdad on autonomy for Kurdistan and political representation in the Baghdad government. Yet, from 1971 to 1980 the Iraqi government expelled more than 200,000 Fayli Kurds (Shias) from Iraq ("History | Unbelievable Kurdistan—Official Tourism Site of Kurdistan" n.d.). In August of 1971, relations between the Kurds and the Iraqi government deteriorated. Mullah Mustafa Barzani appealed to the US for aid (BBC News 2017). In 1972, Iran's Shah asked US President Richard Nixon, to help him support Barzani's uprising against the Iraqi state. Seeing as Iraq was Soviet-aligned, President Nixon agreed to begin supplying the Kurds with weapons (Pitel and Cornish 2019). By 1974 key parts of the agreement were still unfulfilled; plans were not implemented leading to disputes and thus fighting resumed in Iraq in 1974 ("History | Unbelievable Kurdistan—Official Tourism Site of Kurdistan" n.d.) ("The Time of the 11 Kurds" 2017). However, In 1975, the Shah of Iran made a deal with Iraq, cutting out the Kurds and causing their abandonment by the Americans (Pitel and Cornish 2019).

Kurdish Repression—Syria

Meanwhile in Syria, 120,000 Kurds were stripped of citizenship. Per a 1962 census of Syria's Hasakah governorate, any Kurds who could not prove their residency in Syria prior to 1945 and those who failed to participate were stripped of their citizenship, rendering them stateless and unable to travel. One fifth of Syrian Kurds in the largely Kurdish north-east region were stripped of Syrian nationality, barring them from employment, education, civil property rights and political representation. Many lost their land, which the state handed to Arab and Assyrian settlers. Furthermore, these Kurds and their descendants were unable to vote, own property or businesses, or legally marry for decades. In 1970, Syrian leader Hafez al-Assad, a Baathist, seized power, seven years after the party came to power in a coup. In 1973, Assad established an 'Arab belt' along the border of Turkey. This displaced Syrian Kurds from the resource-rich areas in an effort to weaken Kurdish dominance there. In April 2011, amid an intensifying uprising, President Bashar al-Assad promised some "unregistered" Kurds citizenship ("History | Unbelievable Kurdistan—Official Tourism Site of Kurdistan" n.d.) ("The Time of the Kurds" 2017).

Founding the PKK—Turkey

In 1974, The Kurdistan Workers' party (PKK), a radical militant group, was founded by Abdullah Ocalan, a Turkish Kurd, with the aim of creating an independent Kurdish state through violent means (Pitel and Cornish 2019). Abdullah Ocalan founded the Kurdish Workers' Party (PKK) as a Marxist organization with the purpose of establishing an independent Kurdistan in Turkey's southeast. Though initially not seen as a threat, the PKK steadily gained adherents 12 among disenfranchised Kurds. A military coup took place in Turkey in 1980, and the PKK leaders fled to Syria. In 1984, the organization began to use violence against the state and terrorist tactics. Furthermore, the United States designates it as a terrorist organization in 1997. At least forty thousand people have been killed in the Turkish-Kurdish conflict. Kurds have made up the overwhelming majority of victims ("The Time of the Kurds" 2017).

The Algiers Agreement and the Founding of the PUK

In March of 1974, after the fighting reignited in Iraq, the Iraqi government imposed a draft for an autonomy agreement and gave the KDP two weeks to respond. The deal stated the oilfields of Kirkuk would remain under Iraqi government control. Thus, Mullah Mustafa Barzani rejected the agreement, and called for a new rebellion. In 1974, as the Autonomy Agreement crumbled, Iraq's Baathist regime, seeking to consolidate government control over the oil-rich regions in the northern regions of the country, displaced hundreds of thousands of Kurds whom inhabited the area and replaced them with Arabs from central and southern Iraq. Iraqi Kurds, supported by Iran and the United States, revolted against the Baathist regime (BBC News 2017) ("History | Unbelievable Kurdistan—Official Tourism Site of Kurdistan" n.d.) ("The Time of the Kurds" 2017).

In 1975, the Iraqi government signed the Algiers Agreement with Iran, in which Saddam Hussein recognized Iranian sovereignty over half of the Shatt al-Arab estuary in exchange for Shah Mohammad Reza Pahlavi's commitment to stop assisting Iraqi Kurds. The United States, which had been providing money and arms to Iraqi Kurds since 1972 at Iran's request, withdrew its support for the Kurds. The Kurdish rebellion collapsed soon after. At this time, Barzani withdrew from political life ("The Time of the Kurds" 2017) ("Timeline: The Kurds' Quest for Independence" n.d.).

In June of 1975, Jalal Talabani, a former leading member of the KDP, announced the establishment of the Patriotic Union of Kurdistan (PUK) from Damascus (BBC News 2017) ("History | Unbelievable Kurdistan—Official Tourism Site of Kurdistan" n.d.). After the rebellion's collapse, divisions amongst Iraqi Kurds increased. Jalal Talabani denounced Barzani and splintered off from the KDP to establish the Patriotic Union of Kurdistan (PUK). To this day, due to their history, political allegiances between the two parties largely corelate between the two major Kurdish dialects. The PUK established its monopoly in the Sorani-speaking regions of central Iraq while the KDP formed and maintains its center of activity in the northern, Kurmanji-speaking districts ("The Time of the Kurds" 2017).

Massoud Barzani

In 1978, skirmishes broke out between the KDP and the PUK leaving many dead in the wake of them. In 1979, the founder and leader of the KDP, Mullah Mustafa dies. His son, Massoud Barzani, took over the presidency of the Kurdistan Democratic Party of Iraq in March of 1979. He then went on to be elected president of the semiautonomous Kurdistan Regional Government (KRG) in 2005. He held the presidency until 2017 (BBC News 2017) ("The Time of the Kurds" 2017).

Kurds Rebel Following Iran's Islamic Revolution

Kurds were initially supportive of the January 1979 Islamic Revolution, hoping to achieve greater autonomy under Ayatollah Khomeini. However, when their demands went unmet they rebelled against the new regime. Khomeini declared a holy war against the Kurds on August 18, 1979. A military campaign to exert control over Kurdish regions resulted in hundreds of deaths, systematic arrests, and the banning of the Kurdistan Democratic Party of Iran (KDPI) 14 ("The Time of the Kurds" 2017).

Iran–Iraq War, The First Gulf War (1980–1988)

In 1980, the war between Iran and Iraq breaks out, also known as the First Gulf War. The Kurds took up arms in the war. On one side, Iraqi Kurds once again rebelled against Baghdad with Iranian support. On the other, Saddam Hussein enlisted and armed Iranian Kurds. Both governments viewed their country's populations of Kurds as being in league with their enemy and thus each retaliated against civilians. KDP forces worked closely with Iran, but the PUK remained hostile to cooperation with Tehran. Villages were destroyed, and summary executions were common. Existing divisions deepened due to these cross-border alliances; clashes between Iranian and Iraqi Kurds often broke out (BBC News 2017) ("The Time of the Kurds" 2017) ("Timeline: The Kurds' Quest for Independence" n.d.).

In 1983, The Iraqi government kidnapped 8,000 boys and men from the Barzani tribe. In 2005, 500 of them are found in mass graves near the Iraq–Saudi Arabia border, hundreds of kilometers from the Kurdistan Region where they were taken ("History | Unbelievable Kurdistan—Official Tourism Site of Kurdistan" n.d.). Later in 1983 the PUK agreed to a ceasefire with Iraq and began negotiations for Kurdish autonomy. In 1984 in Kurdish northern Iraq, the PKK created it's base to wage a guerrilla war against Turkey. This war has continued on and off for four decades. On one side, the PKK has committed terrorist atrocities; on the other, Turkey arrests and imprisons politically active Kurds and has consistently suppressed the Kurds (Pitel and Cornish 2019). In 1985 the ceasefire between the PUK and Iraq begins to crumble due to increased repression for the Iraqi government.

In 1986, the KDP and PUK reconciled in a meeting held by the Iranian government. Henceforth, the two major Kurdish parties began receiving support from Tehran. From February 15 to September of 1988, as the Iran-Iraq war drew to a close, Hussein and Iraqi forces launched the al-Anfal ("the spoils") campaign, known as the Kurdish Genocide, specifically against Kurdish civilians. Saddam Hussein, the Iraqi president and Ba'athist dictator launched this genocidal campaign against Iraqi Kurds, culminating in a chemical attack on the Kurdish town of Halabja, near the Iranian border. Iraqi government airplanes dropped chemical weapons on the town of Halabja on the 16th and 17th of March 1988. Approximately 5,000 civilians, mostly women and children were killed in a single day. Furthermore, the Anfal campaign consisted of mass executions and disappearances, widespread use of chemical weapons, the destruction of around 2,000 villages, and of the rural economy and infrastructure. In total during the campaign, an estimated of 180,000 Iraqi Kurds, civilians and fighters, were killed and hundreds of thousands were forced into exile, in a systematic attempt to break the Kurdish resistance movement (BBC News 2017) ("History |

Unbelievable Kurdistan—Official Tourism Site of Kurdistan"
n.d.) (Pitel and Cornish 2019) ("The Time of the Kurds"
2017).

No-Fly Zone Enforced Over Iraqi Kurdistan (1991–2003)

In March of 1991, in the days after the Gulf War cease-
fire, US-led forces defeated and expelled Iraqi forces from
Kuwait and the Kurds rebelled against the Iraqi government.
This Kurdish uprising in northern Iraq was encouraged by
the administration of President George HW Bush. However,
Saddam Hussein cracked down on rebelling Iraqi Kurds.
The Iraqi military and helicopters suppressed the uprisings
within weeks. Around 1.5 million Kurds fled before the Iraqi
onslaught, but Turkey closed their border, forcing hundreds
of thousands to seek refuge in the mountains. Tens of thousands of people were internally displaced causing a humanitarian catastrophe. The US, Britain, and France declared
a no-fly zone over Iraqi Kurdistan at the 36th parallel and
provided humanitarian aid in response to the crisis. Months
later, Saddam Hussein 16 withdrew the Iraqi Army and
his administration and imposed an internal blockade on
Kurdistan. Due to the no-fly zone, which remained in place
until the US-led invasion in 2003, and the loss of Iraqi's
government control over the northern regions, Iraqi Kurds
gained de facto autonomy. They elected the first Kurdistan
Regional Government and National Assembly in 1992 (BBC
News 2017) ("History | Unbelievable Kurdistan—Official
Tourism Site of Kurdistan" n.d.) (Pitel and Cornish 2019)
("The Time of the Kurds" 2017).

The Establishment of the Kurdistan Region Government (KRG)

The Iraqi Kurdistan Front, an alliance of political parties, held parliamentary and presidential elections and established the Kurdistan Regional Government (KRG). In May of 1992, elections were held in areas under Kurdish control; KDP candidates gained 50.8% of the vote, while the PUK gained 49.2%. The two parties were equally balanced in the new Kurdish government. In September of the same year, newly established Iraqi National Congress (INC), which brought together a wide-range of Iraqi opposition groups, met in Salah-al-Din in the Kurdish-held north. KDP and PUK representatives take part. In 1994, power-sharing arrangements between the Kurdistan Democratic Party (KDP) and the Patriotic Union of Kurdistan (PUK) fell apart, leading to civil war and two separate administrations, in Erbil and Sulaimaniya respectively (BBC News 2017) ("History | Unbelievable Kurdistan—Official Tourism Site of Kurdistan" n.d.).

Iraqi Kurds Civil War (1994–1998)

The two leading political parties in Iraqi Kurdistan, the Patriotic Union of Kurdistan (PUK), led by Jalal Talabani, and the Kurdistan Democratic Party (KDP), led by Masoud Barzani, fought a civil war in the mid-1990s. This civil war killed more than two thousand Kurds. In 1996, Barzani appealed to Saddam Hussein for assistance as Talabani's PUK received 17 support from Iran. With the help of Iraqi government troops, KDP forces seized the city of Irbil and the PUK stronghold of Sulaymaniyah. A new KDP-led government was created and announced at the parliament building in Irbil. In October of 1996, PUK forces retook Sulaymaniyah and later announced the city as their new government base. Still, both the PUK and KDP claim jurisdiction over the whole of the Kurdish-controlled north. The conflict ended with the U.S.-brokered Washington Peace Agreement on September 17, 1998 when the PUK and KDP signed the Washington Agreement, ending the civil war. Jalal Talabani and Masoud Barzani signed a peace agreement in Washington, but government of the Kurdish region remains split between the two rival administrations (BBC News 2017) ("History | Unbelievable Kurdistan—Official Tourism Site of Kurdistan" n.d.) ("The Time of the Kurds" 2017).

PKK Leader Ocalan Arrested

In 1980, Abdullah Ocalan, leader of Kurdistan Workers' Party (PKK), found refuge in Syria under Hafez Assad's protection. In 1988, under military pressure from Turkey, Syria signed the Adana Agreement committing to end support for the PKK. Ocalan fled. On February 16, 1999 with U.S. help, Ocalan was apprehended by Turkish forces in Nairobi, and was sentenced to life imprisonment for treason. Ocalan's arrest sparked Kurdish protests throughout Turkey and across Europe. Following his capture, the PKK declared a unilateral cease-fire, which ended in June 2004 ("The Time of the Kurds" 2017).

The 2000's

In a letter to the United Nations secretary-general in November of 2000, the PUK accused the Iraqi government of expelling Kurdish families from Kirkuk. In late 2001, fights between the PUK and Jund al-Islam, an Islamic fundamentalist group later renamed Ansar alIslam break out (BBC News 2017). In June of 2002, KDP and PUK leaders held joint discussions 18 with other Iraqi groups aimed at coordinating the work of the opposition in the event of a US-led military campaign against Iraq. In October of that year, a joint session of the Kurdish parliament convened in Irbil. KDP and PUK parliamentarians agreed to work together throughout a transitional session until new elections can be held. In 2003, the US Secretary of State, Colin Powell, accused Iraqi Kurdish Islamist group Ansar al-Islam of playing a pivotal role in linking Osama Bin Ladin's al-Qaeda network with the Iraqi regime. Later that year, Kurdish leaders rejected proposals to bring Turkish troops into northern Iraq as part of a US-led military campaign to oust Saddam Hussein. Anti-Turkish demonstrators took to the streets of Kurdish towns. Furthermore, failure of a parliamentary bill allowing US troops to deploy on Turkish soil hits American plans to open a northern front against Iraq. The Peshmerga, Kurdistan's official armed forces, fought alongside the coalition to liberate Iraq from Saddam Hussein's rule. On March 3, 2003, KDP and PUK created a "joint higher leadership" in the Kurdish-held north, under the chairmanship of the two-party leaders, Massoud Barzani and Jalal Talabani (BBC News 2017) ("History | Unbelievable Kurdistan—Official Tourism Site of Kurdistan" n.d).

Post- Saddam Husein (2003)

The US worked with Iraqi Kurds and the Kurdistan region during the invasion of Iraq. In 2003, the U.S. invasion paved the way for the Kurdistan Regional Government's autonomy. U.S. forces invaded Iraq on March 20, 2003, toppling Saddam Hussein from power. Kurds played a central role in drafting the interim Iraqi constitution, which recognized the autonomy of the Kurdistan Regional Government (KRG) within the new federal system. After the fall of Saddam, the Kurdistan Region of Iraq gained autonomous status and enjoys an economic boom (Pitel and Cornish 2019). Jalal Talabani was named the first Kurdish president of Iraq. Kurdish parties participated in 2005 elections and were included in Prime Minister Nouri al-Maliki's 19 unity government in 2006. The KRG remains a part of the federal Iraqi state through the present ("The Time of the Kurds" 2017).

Syrian Kurds Found PYD

Affiliated with the militant Turkish PKK, the Kurdish Democratic Union Party (PYD) was founded in Syria in 2003. Its platform calls for the recognition of Kurdish rights and regional autonomy. Its loyalty to the PKK puts it at odds with other Syrian Kurdish parties, as well as the Barzani-led Kurdish Regional Government in Iraq ("The Time of the Kurds" 2017).

Turkey Introduces Reforms

Working toward EU membership, Turkey introduced legislative and constitutional reforms in 2003 that expanded Kurdish political and cultural rights, such as permitting the use of the Kurdish language in national television broadcasts. In 2009, Prime Minister Recep Tayyip Erdogan's Justice and Development Party (AKP) government announced a "Kurdish Initiative" with plans for further reforms, which wavered in response to nationalist backlash ("The Time of the Kurds" 2017).

PJAK Emerges in Iran

In 2004, the Party for a Free Life in Kurdistan (PJAK), a PKK-inspired guerrilla group that claimed to have three thousand fighters, takes up arms against the Iranian state. The United States designated PJAK a terrorist organization in 2009 on the basis of its ties to the previously listed PKK. In 2011, PJAK signed a cease-fire agreement with the Iranian government following a massive military campaign that kills hundreds ("The Time of the Kurds" 2017).

Kurds Riot in Syria's Qamishli

In March 2004, after Syrian forces open fire on a procession mourning nine Kurdish youths who died in a brawl between Arabs and Kurds at a soccer match, Syrian Kurds took to the 20 streets in Qamishli. Syrian forces cracked down on the mass demonstrations, yet the protests spread to neighboring towns as well as cities like Aleppo and Damascus, and also inspired demonstrations by Kurds in Europe ("The Time of the Kurds" 2017).

The Beginning of the Kurdistan Regional Government

In a national referendum, Iraqis voted in favor of a new constitution. The new constitution, which was approved by 78 percent of voters, recognized the Kurdistan Region's institutions including the Kurdistan Regional Government and the Kurdistan Parliament. In June of 2005, the first session of Kurdish parliament was held in Irbil; KDP's Massoud Barzani was chosen as president of the newly autonomous region. Later that year, news breaks that a foreign firm had begun drilling for oil in the Kurdish north, sparking new fears of secession among Iraqi Sunni leaders. Kurdish authorities later reported a "major discovery" of oil. In 2006, the PUK and KDP agreed to unify the two administrations. On the 7th May, Prime Minister Nechirvan Barzani announced a new unified cabinet. Later that year, President Massoud Barzani ordered the Iraqi national flag be replaced with the Kurdish one in government buildings. But Iraq's Prime Minister Nuri al-Maliki said, "The Iraqi flag is the only flag that should be raised over any square inch of Iraq" ("History | Unbelievable Kurdistan—Official Tourism Site of Kurdistan" n.d.).

In 2007, Turkish parliament gave its support for military operations in Iraq in pursuit of Kurdish rebels. Turkey faced international pressure and threats of invasion. In the same year, a referendum on whether Kirkuk province should become part of Iraqi Kurdistan was due to be held but is was put on hold indefinitely. In December of 2007, Turkey launched air strikes on fighters from the Kurdish PKK movement inside Iraq. Turkish forces then mounted a ground offensive against PKK Kurdish rebel bases in northern Iraq in 2008. Despite the attacks, Iraqi 21 parliament passed provincial elections law. The city of Kirkuk, claimed by Kurdistan Region, was excluded from provisions of law until its status is settled. In 2009, Turkish warplanes bombed PKK Kurdish rebel positioned in northern Iraq after Turkey accused the group of killing Turkish soldiers in two attacks (BBC News 2017).

In June of 2009, the Kurdish government began crude oil exports to foreign markets. Contractors pump 90,000-100,000 barrels a day from two northern oilfields to Turkey. The central government allowed its pipeline to be used in return for a share of revenues. In July, Massoud Barzani was re-elected as president of the KRG. However, in 2011, protests against corruption and power held by the two parties, the KDP and PUK, started in Sulaymaniyah city. Later that year, Turkey launched air and ground assaults on PKK militants in Iraqi Kurdistan (BBC News 2017).

Syrian Civil War

Furthermore in 2011, The Syrian civil war presented an opportunity for Syrian Kurds to form an autonomous administration in north-east Syria. The US choose experienced Kurdish fighters of the PKK-aligned People's Protection Units (YPG) to spearhead the fight in northeast Syria against the Islamic State, Sunni jihadis who have taken advantage of the power vacuum to seize control of a vast territory across Syria and Iraq (Pitel and Cornish 2019). Amid the escalating uprisings, Syrian President Bashar al-Assad, seeking to court Kurdish support, issued Decree 49 in

2011, granting citizenship to Kurds who were registered as foreigners in the 1962 census. Yet, Kurds who were never registered remain stateless. On November 12, 2013, the Kurds declared autonomy in Kurdish held Northern Syria. Amid the ongoing civil war, the Kurdish PYD established three de facto autonomous cantons in Syria's north known as Rojava (Western Kurdistan), and unilaterally declared autonomy ("The Time of the Kurds" 2017).

Turkey and the KRG Grow Closer

Reversing earlier policy, Turkey deepened ties and energy cooperation with Iraqi Kurds following the U.S. withdrawal from Iraq. In April 2011, Prime Minister Erdogan becomes the first Turkish leader to visit Iraqi Kurdistan in April 2011, followed by a historic visit by KRG President Masoud Barzani to Diyarbakir, in southeastern Turkey, on November 16, 2013. Meanwhile, in May 2012, the parties agreed to build three pipelines to bring oil and gas from the KRG to Turkey ("The Time of the Kurds" 2017). Also, in 2012, Turkey and the PKK renewed peace talks. Direct official negotiations between the Turkish government and jailed PKK leader Abdullah Ocalan seek to bring an end to three decades of conflict, which had killed forty thousand people. Secret negotiations in Oslo began in 2009 were revealed when a tape was leaked in 2011 (BBC News 2017) ("The Time of the Kurds" 2017).

KRG 2013-2014: Political Shifts and Oil

In 2013 an influx of refugees from Syria prompted KRG authorities to shut the border temporarily in May. In August, President Barzani secured a two-year extension to his second term of office. The next month, regional parliamentary elections majorly shifted as the opposition Change Movement party won 24 seats, pushing Iraqi President Jalal Talabani's Patriotic Union of Kurdistan (PUK) into third place. The Kurdistan Democratic Party (KDP) of regional President Massoud Barzani remained the largest bloc with 38 seats (BBC News 2017). Furthermore, in 2013, the KRG bypassed Baghdad to sell oil. Iraqi Kurdistan began direct energy exports, and bypassed Iraqi government by avoiding paying Baghdad the cut it demands of the KRG's sales. This action raised concerns in Baghdad and Washington that the oil revenue would allow Kurds to seek independence. In a sign of warming relations, Turkey was among the KRG's oil buyers.

In March of 2014, Iraqi government under Prime Minister Nuri al-Maliki retaliated by blocking the transfer of the KRG's 17 percent share of federal revenues, leaving regional leaders unable to pay the salaries of officials and leading to a fiscal crisis for the Kurdish region. In May, Kurdistan officially marketed its first pipeline oil, despite opposition from the government in Baghdad. In June, ISIS (The Islamic State in Iraq and the Levant) seized control of much of Anbar Province and approached Baghdad, Kurdish Peshmerga forces captured Kirkuk—the oil rich city outside the borders of Iraqi Kurdistan that Iraqi Kurds have long regarded as their capital. In July, KRG President Barzani announced plans for an independence referendum later in the year.

In December of 2014, the Iraqi government and the Kurdish leadership signed a deal agreeing to share Iraq's oil wealth and military resources. The KRG recommitted to sell oil through Iraq's national oil-marketing company in exchange for renewed federal revenue sharing. This deal fueled hopes that the agreement would help to reunite the country in the face of the common threat represented by Islamic State (BBC News 2017) ("The Time of the Kurds" 2017).

Rise of Islamic State

In 2014, aiming to establish a caliphate in the Levant, the self-proclaimed Islamic State, a Sunni Muslim jihadi group, took control of large swaths of Iraq in 2014, including Mosul, Iraq's second-largest city, and territory controlled by the semiautonomous KRG. Iraqi national forces and the KRG's Peshmerga buckled in the face of Islamic State advances. However, in June the Peshmerga took control of the long-disputed, oil-rich city Kirkuk. In August, the Islamic State conquered several Kurdish-held towns. In response, the United States jets supported Kurdish Peshmerga forces by striking jihadist positions. The United States and Iraqi governments supplied Peshmerga fighters with weapons to help them battle Islamists. Iraqi government 24 shifted majorly as Iraqi Prime Minister Nuri al-Maliki, who had come to be seen as an increasingly divisive figure who alienated the Kurds, is replaced by Haider al-Abadi. In September, Kurdish leaders agreed to put the referendum for independence on hold as they focus fighting the Islamic State on the ground. In October, Islamic State militants attacked Kobani, a strategically located northern Syrian Kurdish town that borders

Turkey and was controlled by the Democratic Union Party (PYD), the leading political party among Syrian Kurds and the Syrian branch of the Kurdistan Workers Party (PKK). The Iraqi Kurdistan government sent Peshmerga forces to Kobani, via Turkey, to back fellow Kurdish fighters attempting to defend the city from attack by Islamic State militants. The PYD's effective defense led the United States to come to its support with heavy airstrikes and parachute drops of armaments. However, U.S. support for the PKK's affiliate resulted in a crisis in U.S.-Turkey relations (BBC News 2017) ("The Time of the Kurds" 2017).

Turkey joined the fight against the Islamic State but insisted that air-strikes against IS should be paired with operations against Kurdish PKK militants in northern Iraq. Turkey began bombing the Islamic State's positions in Syria, while Turkey granted the United States access to its Incirlik air base to support air raids on Islamic State targets. At the same time, Turkey also launched bombing campaigns and attacked PKK targets in Iraqi Kurdistan, the first time that it had attacked the Kurds since reaching a ceasefire with them in 2013. Thus, ending a two-year cease-fire. In 2015, the faltering peace process between the PKK and the Turkish state collapsed and led to a surge in violence. Urban warfare erupted in cities across Turkey's Kurdish majority south-east and a wave of PKK-linked bombings hit cities to the west, including the capital Ankara and Istanbul. The breakdown in the talks, that had been spearheaded by Turkish president Recep Tayyip Erdogan and accompanied by reforms aimed at improving Kurdish 25 rights, was followed by a wave of arrests of Kurdish activists and politicians (BBC News 2017) ("The Time of the Kurds" 2017) (Pitel and Cornish 2019).

KRG Constitutional Reform, Political Tensions, Financial Crisis

In May of 2015, Iraqi Kurdistan parliament appointed a committee to oversee revisions of their constitution. One of the issues under review was the number of terms the president should be allowed to serve. In June, President Barzani's chief of staff announced that a presidential election would be held on August 20th, a day after President Barzani's then current term of office expired. The president's critics accused him of seeking to preempt any revision to the constitution that would have prevented him from serving a further term. In August, President Barzani's extended term in office ends. However, he was given another two years while the opposing party claimed the move to do so is illegal. In October, a key Change Movement leader was expelled from coalition government following days of violent street protests against President Barzani. Parliament was suspended. In September 2015, the United States ruled in favor of an Iraqi government bid to block Kurdish oil sales to a US buyer. In February 2016, the KRG cuts the pay of public service employees to tackle a deepening financial crisis June, the KRG's financial crisis worsens and the KRG threatened to cut water supplies from the Tigris River to the rest of Iraq after Baghdad buys smaller than expected quantities of wheat products from Kurdistan (BBC News 2017).

The Kurds and the War against the Islamic State

The Kurds have featured heavily on all fronts of the battle against ISIS. In April 2016, the United States began paying salaries of the Kurdish Peshmerga fighters fighting against the Islamic State. In June, Peshmerga forces reported increasing use of "chemical weapons" by IS and pled for more weapons for fight the militants. Thus, in July, the United States and the 26 Kurdistan Regional Government signed a memo of understanding in which Washington agrees to provide more military aid to Peshmerga forces. This move deeply angered Baghdad. Furthermore, in August, Germany resumed direct shipment of weapons to Iraqi Kurdistan after regional government pledged to prevent the weapons from ending up on the black market (BBC News 2017).

The same month, Turkey intervened in Syria. After years of supporting Syrian rebels, Turkey intervened directly in northern Syria, backing Arab fighters against the Islamic State. Partly motivated so Turkey could restrict Syrian Kurds from connecting their two cantons, and that goal was largely successful during the seven-month operation. The Turkish deployment of troops and advisors halted a Kurdish advance west of the Euphrates river and created a complex frontline that included the two opposing U.S. allies and Russian and Iranian backed forces loyal to the Assad regime ("The Time of the Kurds" 2017).

On May 9, 2017, the U.S. arms Syrian Kurds. US President Donald Trump approved a plan to arm the Syrian Democratic Forces (SDF), the militia dominated by the YPG. The plan entailed directly arming Syrian Kurds via the Defense Department as the U.S.-led coalition against the Islamic State prepared to seize Raqqa. This move further angered Turkey, as Turkey had previously tried and failed, to promote its proxy wars and agendas to take the lead in Raqqa ("The Time of the Kurds" 2017).

KRG Increased Oil Activity and the Kurdish Flag

In December 2016, the KRG stated it will not abide by the OPEC agreement to reduce oil production to help cut Iraq's overall oil output. The United States oil giant Exxon Mobil pulled out of half of the six exploration blocks it operated across Iraqi Kurdistan. In January 2017. Russian oil company Gazprom Neft, the third largest oil producer in Russia, moved to increase 27 oil extraction in Iraqi Kurdistan despite the security threat posed by the Islamic State. Later that year, Russia's Rosneft reportedly paid one billion US dollars in advance for Iraqi Kurdistan's crude oil, signaling increasing Russian interest in the Kurdistan region's natural resources (BBC News 2017).

In February 2017, President Barzani visited Turkey and Turkey raised the Kurdistan Regional Government's flag during his visit. The following month, the governor of the disputed city of Kirkuk ordered the Kurdistan regional flag to be flown over all government buildings, drawing condemnation from Baghdad as well as Iran and Turkey. Turkey opposed this move despite having flown the flag themselves the previous month. Tukey continued to purchase Kurdish oil while moving to separate Kurdish forces fighting the Islamic state, highlighting the Kurds and Turkey's complicated relationship. Furthermore, in April 2017, Turkish jets carried out deadly air strikes on Peshmerga forces positioned near Sinjar in Iraq and Syrian Kurdish fighters across the border in Syria (BBC News 2017).

KRG Referendum for Independence

In June 2017, A bipartisan meeting led by President Barzani agreed to hold an independence referendum on September 25th of the same year. The provincial council of the disputed city of Kirkuk votes to take part in the referendum. However, many prominent Kurds launch the "No for now" movement, which claimed it would be wrong to hold a referendum under current security and economic conditions, namely ISIS and the KRG's budget cuts and financial crisis. However, the independence referendum went ahead in the face of international opposition. On September 25, 2017 Iraqi Kurds voted for independence. Voters in Iraqi Kurdistan overwhelmingly voted yes for independence in a referendum held by regional officials despite the objections of the Iraqi government.

Baghdad rejected attempts to break up the state and especially the KRG's insistence on holding the vote in the disputed territory of oil-rich Kirkuk. While KRG President Barzani hoped a resounding "yes" vote would bolster the KRG in negotiations with Baghdad over separating from Iraq, the central government refused talks and instead Baghdad moved to assert its authority and imposed punitive measures, further isolating the region, followed by similar moves of opposition by Iran, Syria, and Turkey. The next month, President Barzani resigned (BBC News 2017) ("The Time of the Kurds" 2017). Barzani had led the KRG since it was established in 2005, as it's only president until his resignation. His second term expired in 2013 but was extended, under dispute and illegally, without elections being held due as the Islamic State moved in major regions of territory in Iraq and Syria (Chmaytelli 2017).

Barzani announced his resignation and said that he would officially step down as president on November 1st, stating the move came from the pressure from the United States and other international powers. Though his extended presidency was illegal, in his resignation letter, Barzani stressed that "…it is not permissible to amend the law of the presidency of the region, it must be suspended until the next election and the fifth session of the parliament, and work must stop on any laws that contradict this message." He handed over majority of the powers of the presidency to the Prime Minister, his nephew Nechirvan Barzani. However, after Barzani's resignation the question remained over who would succeed him. Nechirvan Barzani later was elected president and currently still holds the office (Abdullah 2018).

Ongoing Fight Against the Islamic State

On March 17, 2018, Turkish troops captured Syrian Kurdish held cities. The battles lasted a month and resulted in dozens of civilian deaths; President Recep Tayyip Erdogan said Turkish forces and allied Syrian rebels had gained "total control" of Afrin, a city in northern 29 Syria previously held by YPG forces. According to the United Nations, tens of thousands of civilians fled their homes during this time, worsening the already historic refugee crisis ("The Time of the Kurds" 2017). In December 2018, US President Donald Trump made his first threat to withdraw US troops from the fight against ISIS, claiming the jihadis had been defeated. He moderates his position to a partial drawdown after a furious backlash in the US and abroad at the abandoning of the Kurds who have been allies of the US in combating the extremists in northeast Syria.

In 2019, the Syrian Democratic Forces, both Kurdish fighters and Arab groups opposed to President Bashar al-Assad's regime, finally won major territorial victory over ISIS in northeast Syria with backing from an international coalition led by the US (Pitel and Cornish 2019). On March 23, 2019 Syrian Kurds declared victory over ISIS. The SDF took control of areas around the town of Baghouz, near the Iraq-Syria border, the last populated area held by the Islamic State. An SDF spokesperson declared the "total elimination," and U.S. officials say it marks the end of the Islamic State's territorial rule. Yet, other leaders in the region warned that Islamic State fighters still pose a threat ("The Time of the Kurds" 2017).

On October 6, 2019, the U.S. announced troop withdrawal from the fight. US President Trump announced a plan to remove U.S. troops from Syria, breaking the news through his Twitter account. Troops withdrew from the Turkey-Syria border where US forces had been conducting joint patrols with Turkey as part of a mechanism to reassure Ankara that separatist Kurdish fighters would not use the area to attack Turkey. President Trump's decision to remove troops has widely been seen standing aside to allow the long-threatened Turkish military advance into this territory, pitting America's Kurdish allies against an enemy they consider a greater 30 threat than ISIS (Pitel and Cornish 2019). The withdrawal of US troops did indeed clear the way for the Turkish military to launch a long-threatened offensive against Kurdish forces in the area.

Conclusion

The estimated population of thirty million Kurds resides primarily in mountainous regions of present-day

Iran, Iraq, Syria, and Turkey and remain the world's largest people group without a sovereign state. Since the fall of the Ottoman Empire, Kurds have been dispersed into the above four nations for nearly a century. They have pursued recognition, political rights, autonomy, and independence. Throughout this period, Kurds have been persecuted, Kurdish identity has been denied, and thousands of Kurds have been killed. In each of the four nations of Turkey, Syria, Iraq, and Iran, Kurds have had uneasy relationships with authorities, at times rebelling and at other times cutting deals with the governments. The destabilization of Iraq, civil war in Syria, and the rise, and collapse, of the Islamic State presented new challenges, but also opportunities, for the Kurds and their fairly recent autonomous government in Northern Iraq ("The Time of the Kurds" 2017).

CHAPTER 2

Regional Relationships and Current Events

Introduction

In this chapter I will cover the Kurd's relationships with their neighbors in the Middle East, specifically the Kurdistan Regional Government of Iraq's relationship with Turkey, Syria, Iraq, and Syria. I will also further touch on the current status of the KRG's standing and relationships in the region. I will highlight these relationships in the Middle East in both historical and current context; there will be some recap from the previous chapter to add further context to current events, but this chapter will be more topical focused rather than chronological like the previous one was. Domestic upheaval and political changes throughout the region have made Kurds critical players on many fronts. Intertwined conflicts are still at play and very much factoring into their current status and future hope for independence.

Battling the Islamic State

Kurds in both Iraq and Syria continue to fight against the Islamic State, though the battle is waning. Thousands of Kurds have been killed in battles that shrunk the Islamic State's footprint to a fraction of its 2014 peak, a sacrifice which has earned the Kurds a global reputation as the most effective ground forces against the militant group. The United States trained Iraqi Kurds and backed Syrian Kurds with airpower, though notably, it refused to circumvent Baghdad and directly provide arms to the Peshmerga. Iraqi Kurds received training and weapons from European countries, as well as Iran. Support from foreign powers raised concerns in Iraq, which is wary of further empowering its autonomous Kurdish region. As the battle against the Islamic State winds down, Kurds have solidifying control over large parts of their respective countries. However, their success may end up being short-lived due to the removal of U.S. troops and 32 waning support as both Turkey and Syria continue to focus on squashing the potential for an autonomous Kurdish state ("The Time of the Kurds" 2017).

In mid-2013, the jihadist group Islamic State turned its sights on three Kurdish enclaves that bordered territory under its control in northern Syria. It launched repeated attacks that until mid-2014 were repelled by the People's Protection Units (YPG), the armed branch of the Syrian Kurdish Democratic Union Party (PYD). The Islamic State advanced in northern Iraq in June 2014, further drawing Iraq's Kurds into the conflict. The government of Iraq's autonomous Kurdistan Region sent its Peshmerga forces to areas abandoned by the Iraqi army. In August 2014, the jihadists launched a surprise offensive and the Peshmerga withdrew from several areas. A number of towns inhabited by religious minorities fell, notably Sinjar, where IS militants killed or captured thousands of Yazidis, a minority religious group primarily made up of Kurds (BBC News 2019).

In September 2014, IS launched an assault on the enclave around the northern Syrian Kurdish town of Kobani, forcing tens of thousands of people to flee across the nearby Turkish border. Despite the proximity of the fighting, Turkey refused to attack IS positions or allow Turkish Kurds to cross to defend it. Kurds accused Turkish authorities of complicity. In response, a US-led multinational coalition launched air strikes in northern Iraq and sent military advisers to help the Peshmerga. The YPG and the Kurdistan Workers' Party (PKK), which has fought for Kurdish autonomy in Turkey for three decades and has bases in Iraq, also came to their aid. Eventually, In January 2015, after a battle that left at least 1,600 people dead, Kurdish forces regained control of Kobani (BBC News 2019). The Kurds, fighting alongside several local Arab militias, under the banner of the Syrian Democratic Forces alliance, and helped by US-led coalition air strikes, weapons and advisers steadily drove IS out of tens of thousands of square 33 kilometers of territory in north-eastern Syria and established control over a large stretch of the border with Turkey. In October 2017, SDF fighters captured the de facto IS capital of Raqqa and then advanced south-eastwards into the neighboring province of Deir al-Zour—the jihadists' last major foothold in Syria. (BBC News 2019).

The last pocket of territory held by IS in Syria, around the village of Baghouz, fell to the Kurds of the SDF in March 2019. Though the SDF acclaimed the total elimination of the IS caliphate, it warned that jihadist sleeper cells remained a threat. The SDF was left responsible to deal with the thousands of suspected IS militants captured during the last two years of the battle, as well as tens of thousands of displaced women and children associated with IS fighters. The US called for the repatriation of foreign nationals among them, but most of their home countries refused. Furthermore, in October 2019, US troops were removed from the border with Turkey after the country's president said it was about to launch an operation to set up a 32km (20-mile) deep "safe zone" clear of YPG fighters and resettle up to 2 million Syrian refugees there. The SDF said it was betrayed by the US and warned that the offensive might reverse the defeat of the Islamic State (BBC News 2019). This furthered the Kurd's feelings of betrayal from the US and other allies. The Kurds are still battling the remnants of ISIS while defending themselves against the neighboring hostile regimes.

Turkey

When it comes to the Kurd's relationship with Turkey, it is vital to note that Turkey sees their current borders as the rightful ones while the Kurds hold to the Treaty of Sèvres, which outlined an independent Kurdistan, but was never implemented. Turkey, like other Middle Eastern countries with Kurdish minorities, sees Kurdish nationalism as a threat to its national security and to the modern borders drawn up after World War I. This fear is more acute in 34 Turkey than other countries, due to the fact that one-fifth of Turkey's population, about 12 million people, are Kurds. Turkey has long considered Kurds to be merely "Mountain Turks." A ban on speaking Kurdish in Turkey has been lifted and Kurdish broadcasts there are now legal, yet other expressions of Kurdish culture are restricted (BBC News 2019) (Bruno 2007). Kurds and Turkey have a long history of conflict and

Kurds have historically been more suppressed by Turkey than any other regional power.

Though most of the conflict between Kurds and Turkey are internal—Turkish Kurds and the Turkish government—Turkey and the Kurdistan Regional Government have a complicated relationship. Turkey is one of the main purchasers of Kurdistan's oil. The KRG is largely dependent on these oil sales and Turkish ports for sales. In this way, their relationship is beneficial. However, Turkey is completely against the KRG, or Kurds anywhere, attaining independence or sovereignty as they see this as a threat to their own government and territory.

Kurdish Suppression

Kurds received harsh treatment at the hands of the Turkish authorities for generations. In response to uprisings in the 1920s and 1930s, many Kurds were resettled, Kurdish names and costumes were banned, the use of the Kurdish language was restricted, and even the existence of a Kurdish ethnic identity was denied, with people designated "Mountain Turks" (BBC News 2019). It wasn't until recently that Kurdish languages were even legal in the nation. Turkey's decades of suppression is a major factor causing the Kurd's general lack of ethnic identity and development. The restrictions imposed on Kurds barred language and cultural development as well as education and business expansion.

Internal Conflict and The PKK

There is deep-seated hostility between the Turkish state and the country's Kurds, who constitute 15% to 20% of the population (BBC News 2019) ("Factbox: The Kurdish Struggle for Rights and Land" 2019). A major factor as to why Turkey views Kurds as a threat is the Kurdistan Workers Party (PKK), which has Marxist-Leninist roots. The PKK was formed in the late 1970s and launched an armed struggle against the Turkish government in 1984. The PKK has been fighting for an independent Kurdish state within Turkey since, especially waging an insurgency for autonomy in Turkey's largely Kurdish southeast (BBC News 2016).

Though a shift came in the 1990s, when the PKK rolled back on its demands for an independent state, calling instead for more autonomy for the Kurds, it did little to ease relational tensions. In a BBC interview in April 2016, the PKK's military leader said the group does not "want to separate from Turkey and set up a state...but want to live within the borders of Turkey on our own land freely. The struggle will continue until the Kurds' innate rights are accepted. Turkey continues to accuse the PKK of trying to create a separate state in Turkey" (BBC News 2016). Either way, the conflict between the PKK and Turkey has been a violent one and over 40,000 people have died in the conflict (BBC News 2016) (BBC News 2019).

Some observers blame the United States for supporting separatists. The newly found autonomy enjoyed by Iraqi Kurds in the KRG following the fall of Saddam Hussein has encouraged the PKK. The Turks previously held back from retaliation, largely because they hoped that America would deal with the PKK. So far, that hasn't happened (Bruno 2007). In fact, before troops withdrew from the region, the

United States was providing assistance on the ground for the Kurds more than anyone else in the region. However, the United States, the European Union and Turkey classify the PKK as a terrorist organization (BBC News 2016) ("Factbox: The Kurdish Struggle for Rights and Land" 2019).

The fragile peace process between the Turkish government and the outlawed Kurdish insurgent group, the PKK, is broken, and both sides appear entrenched in a violent struggle that most analysts say can't be resolved militarily. The Turkish army is one of the world's largest, but Kurdish militias have proven resilient and their fighters, if not their cause, have gained international recognition after successes against the Islamic State. Tensions have been exacerbated by the conflicts in Iraq and Syria. The Turkish military has driven out PKK fighters from urban centers and has targeted the group and other militants in Syria and Iraq, earning rebukes from rights groups for alleged abuses in its domestic operations and from the United States for impeding the campaign against the Islamic State ("The Time of the Kurds" 2017).

Kurds and Turkey: Conclusion

Kurds in Turkey have repeatedly taken to the streets in protest of the Turkish government. The Kurds felt the government of Turkey sees the Kurds as the real enemy more so than the Islamic State and therefore blocked Kurds from aiding the autonomous entity in Syria (BBC News 2014). Though Turkey's President, Tayyip Erdogan, had removed restrictions on using the Kurdish language, the Kurds still experience suppression from Ankara. The government held talks with Ocalan, the PPK founder who is in jail on an island near Istanbul, in 2012, but the talks broke down and the conflict has since revived ("Factbox: The Kurdish Struggle for Rights and Land" 2019). South-eastern Turkey has been wracked by violence since the ceasefire with the PKK collapsed. The Turkish air force now regularly carries out air strikes against PKK bases in mountainous northern Iraq. The Turkish government has stated they refuse to engage in any negotiations until the group completely disarms (BBC News 2016).

Syria

Before Syria's uprising and civil war erupted in 2011, eight to ten percent of the population of Syria was made up of Kurds ("Factbox: The Kurdish Struggle for Rights and Land" 2019). Historically, the Baathist movement and party, championing Arab nationalism, had deprived thousands of Kurds of citizenship rights, banned their language and clamped down on Kurdish political activity. During the war, President Bashar al-Assad focused on crushing mainly Sunni Arab rebels with the help of Russia and Iran, turning a blind eye and allowing Kurdish fighters to seize self-rule across regions in the north and east of Syria. Kurdish forces have emerged among the biggest winners, controlling about a quarter of the country—territory rich in oil, water and farmland. It is the biggest chunk of Syria not in state hands, now with its own forces and bureaucracy ("Factbox: The Kurdish Struggle for Rights and Land" 2019).

Syrian Kurds

Before the uprising against President Bashar al-Assad began in 2011, most Kurds lived in the cities of Damascus and Aleppo, and in three, non-contiguous areas around Kobane, Afrin, and the north-eastern city of Qamishli. Syria's Kurds have long been suppressed and denied basic rights. Some 300,000 have been denied citizenship since the 1960s, and Kurdish land has been confiscated and redistributed to Arabs in an attempt to "Arabize" Kurdish regions. When the uprising evolved into a civil war, the main Kurdish parties publicly avoided taking sides. In mid2012, government forces withdrew to concentrate on fighting the rebels elsewhere, and Kurdish groups took control in their absence (BBC News 2019).

The Partiya Yekîtiya Demokrat, the Democratic Union Party (PYD), is the dominant force in Syria's Kurdish regions. The Yekîneyên Parastina Gel (YPG) is essentially the military branch of PYD, the Syrian affiliate of the PKK. The YPG emerged as a key ally of the US-led 38 coalition battle against IS (BBC News 2019). Furthermore, the Kurdish YPG militia's power grew after joining forces with U.S. troops to seize territory from Islamic State. While the U.S. deployment had provided a security umbrella that helped Kurdish influence expand, the U.S. maintained its opposition of any autonomy plans. However, Syrian Kurdish leaders say they do not seek partition but rather regional autonomy as part of Syria ("Factbox: The Kurdish Struggle for Rights and Land" 2019).

In January 2014, Kurdish parties, including the dominant Democratic Union Party, declared the creation of "autonomous administrations" in the three "cantons" of Afrin, Kobani, and Jazira. In March 2016, they announced the establishment of a "federal system" that included mainly Arab and Turkmen areas captured from IS. The declaration was rejected by the Syrian government, Syrian opposition, Turkey and the US. Though the PYD claims it is not seeking independence, the PYD insists that any political settlement to end the conflict in Syria must include legal guarantees for Kurdish rights and recognition of Kurdish autonomy (BBC News 2019).

President Assad has vowed to retake "every inch" of Syrian territory, whether by negotiations or military force. His government has also rejected Kurdish demands for autonomy, saying that "nobody in Syria accepts talk about independent entities or federalism" (BBC News 2019). For over three years, the Kurdish-dominated Syrian Democratic Forces had fought alongside US troops in the battle against the Islamic State. However, US President Trump's shift in US policies and his decision to pull troops out, left them vulnerable to an attack by Turkey. Fighting is still happening today. Kurds often say they have "no friends but the mountains,", alluding to a long history of betrayal. This narrative continues today (Pitel and Cornish 2019)."

The Kurds and Syria: Conclusion

Syrian Kurds have faced extreme opposition and suppression from the Syrian government. It wasn't until recently they were allowed citizenship and the right to speak their own language. They are still suppressed but have gained ground in some northern regions. Syrian Kurds were most effected by the removal of US troops and are currently fighting to protect their small region from an oppressive regime and the Islamic State. Though the US president has claimed the fight against ISIS is over, it is nowhere near so for Syrian Kurds.

Iran

In Iran, Kurds form about ten percent of the population. In 2011, Iran pledged to step up military action against the Party of Free Life of Kurdistan, a PKK offshoot that has sought greater autonomy for Kurds in Iran. Rights groups say Kurds, along with other religious and ethnic minorities, face discrimination under the ruling clerical establishment. The elite Revolutionary Guards have put down unrest in the Kurdish community for decades, and the country's judiciary has sentenced many activists to long jail terms or death. Iran's military has demanded Iraqi authorities' hand over separatist Kurdish dissidents stationed there and close their bases ("Factbox: The Kurdish Struggle for Rights and Land" 2019). Kurds in Iran receive less attention than those in the surrounding nations, though they still aim to achieve greater rights from the state (Zanotti and Thomas 2019).

Iranian-backed paramilitaries and Kurdish fighters fought alongside each other to defeat Islamic State. Since the US pulled out and ISIS was pushed out of previously held regions, the alliance has faltered. Iran threatened military actions after the Kurdistan Regional Government's independence referendum (Chmaytelli 2017). Iranian armed forces conducted a significant military drill on the border between Iran and Iraq as Tehran warned the Kurds not to move 40 forward with the plebiscite (Tabatabai 2017). In conclusion, Iran is just as much against Kurdish independence as the rest of the region.

Iraq

The Kurds make up an estimated fifteen to twenty percent of Iraq's population (BBC News 2019) ("Factbox: The Kurdish Struggle for Rights and Land" 2019). They have historically enjoyed more national rights than Kurds living in neighboring states, but also faced brutal repression (BBC News 2019). The Kurds have been suppressed by the government of Iraq just as they have been by other regional governments. Furthermore, the Kurds faced horrors under the late President Saddam Hussein's rule. Yet, it was his downfall that ultimately led to Iraqi Kurds gaining autonomy in the region. The Kurdistan Region Government has been semi-autonomous since 1991.

Kurds Under Saddam Hussein's Regime

The Kurds have historically faced a lot of discrimination, suppression, and violence from all neighboring nations including Iraq, but none has been worse than that which the Kurds experienced during the reign of Saddam Hussein. The dictator's response to a Kurdish rebellion was to commit mass genocide. Rather than granting the Kurds autonomy when they rebelled for it, Saddam lined up Kurdish civilians and executed them. Hussein targeted Iraqi Kurds in the late 1980s with chemical gas. Villages were razed and thousands of Kurds were forced into camps. This became known as the Anfal campaign. Saddam cruelly named his slaughter after a verse in the Koran. Somewhere between 50,000 to 180,000 Kurdish civilian lives were claimed during this campaign (Beauchamp 2014) ("Factbox: The Kurdish Struggle for Rights and Land" 2019).

The Establishment of The Kurdistan Region Government

When Iraq was defeated in the 1991 Gulf War, Barzani's son Massoud and Jalal Talabani of the rival Patriotic Union of Kurdistan (PUK) led a Kurdish rebellion. However, Saddam viciously put them down. The international community didn't stop Saddam, but it did intervene after the fact to set up a "safe zone" for Kurds in part of Kurdistan, where they could live in peace without fear of Saddam's army. The US and its allies imposed a no-fly zone in the north that allowed Kurds to enjoy self-rule. Kurdish militias eventually expanded the zone to what it is today, and the Kurds set up a government with de facto autonomy. The US invaded in 2003, toppled Saddam, and replaced him with a government that formalized the Kurdish semiautonomous government. The parties co-operated with the US-led invasion in 2003 that toppled Saddam and governed in coalition in the Kurdistan Regional Government. Massoud Barzani's KDP and Jalal Talabani's PUK shared power after the fall of Saddam, it was tumultuous at times and led to a few years of civil war (BBC News 2019) (Beauchamp 2014).

The Kurdistan Regional Government

The KRG has its own regional government, foreign policy, and armed forces, but still relies on the Iraqi central government for its budget and federal funding. Yet, in practice, Kurds have more autonomy in reality than what they technically have on paper. Iraqi Kurdistan is defined as the three provinces: Dohuk, Erbil, and Sulaymaniyah. The KRG functions as a confederal region, not a federal one.

For example, Iraqi Kurdistan is more autonomous than an American state, but is still not quite its own country—yet. However, Iraqi Kurdistan is the closest thing to a Kurdish state ("Factbox: The Kurdish Struggle for Rights and Land" 2019) (Beauchamp 2014).

Iraq and The KRG

In the past decade, Iraq's authority has weakened. The Iraqi central government's control over its borders and border crossings have considerably weakened, especially since the fall of the Ba'ath regime in 2003. Furthermore, when Islamic State militants swept through much of northern Iraq in 2014, Kurdish fighters exploited the collapse of central authority to take control of Kirkuk, the oil city they regard as their ancient regional capital, as well as other territory disputed by Baghdad and the Kurdish north. Iraqi government forces and Kurdish Peshmerga fighters, with U.S. backing, defeated Islamic State which had captured swathes of northern Iraq. As the fragile state of Iraq directed its resources and manpower toward securing central areas of Iraq and other strategically vital locations, several border areas and geographic peripheries became places of chaos, anarchy, and contestation by local groups, foreign powers, criminal organizations, and insurgents. Kurdistan seized what control they could over some borders. Today, the two main Kurdish parties, the Kurdistan Democratic Party and the Patriotic Union of Kurdistan, have de facto control over Kurdistan's border crossings with Turkey and Iran ("Factbox: The Kurdish Struggle for Rights and Land" 2019) (Hasan 2019).

Iraqi Kurdish Independence

People in Kurdish-held areas decisively backed independence in a September 2017 referendum. More than 90% of the 3.3 million people who voted supported secession. Officials of the Kurdistan Regional Government said the result gave them a mandate to start negotiations with Baghdad, yet, then Iraqi Prime Minister Haider al-Abadi demanded that it be annulled. The following month Iraqi pro-government forces retook the disputed territory held by the Kurds. The loss of Kirkuk and its oil revenue was a major blow to Kurdish aspirations for their own state (BBC News 2019).

The September 2017 referendum on independence was overwhelmingly backed by Iraqi Kurdish voters. However, it raised tensions with surrounding countries. Ultimately the referendum backfired and triggered a regional crisis in the face of opposition from Baghdad and regional powers. The vote prompted military and economic retaliation from Baghdad. Relations have since improved, but tensions remain over oil exports and revenue-sharing. While the Kurdish government framed the vote as a mandate to negotiate with Baghdad over the terms of separation, then Prime Minister Haider al-Abadi instead demanded that the referendum be annulled and threatened to isolate the landlocked region. A move toward independence would also risk conflict with Iran-backed Shia militias and possibly even inflame the sectarian competition between Iraq's Sunni and Shia Arabs (BBC News 2019) ("Factbox: The Kurdish Struggle for Rights and Land" 2019) ("The Time of the Kurds" 2017).

Neighboring Iran, Syria, and Turkey are concerned that independence for Iraq's Kurds could inspire uprisings in their own countries. In addition, regional and international powers are concerned that an independent Iraqi Kurdistan would harbor militants. Under Erdogan, Turkey has forged extensive economic ties with the KRG, including a booming oil trade, but also targeted PKK posts in KRG territory in 2017. After the referendum, Turkey threatened to shut down an oil pipeline on which the KRG relies. This furthered the KRG's financial crisis ("The Time of the Kurds" 2017).

International support is seen as critical to the viability of an independent Kurdistan since it would be landlocked and reliant on its neighbors for the passage of goods and people. Iraqi Kurds moved forward with the September referendum, experts say, because they fear that U.S. support for them will only dry up as the campaign against the Islamic State winds down. But even so, the United States condemned the referendum, reiterating its commitment to a unified 44 federal Iraq and reflecting the concerns of Turkey, a NATO ally. The European Union, too, called the vote illegitimate. Additional countries have also been reluctant to support Kurdish independence due to minority secessionist movements within their own borders ("The Time of the Kurds" 2017).

A month after the referendum and after his gamble on the vote backfired, in a televised address on October 29, 2017, the president of the Iraqi Kurdish region, Masoud Barzani, announced that he would be stepping down from his post. Disagreements between the main parties caused the post to remain vacant until June 2019, when former President Masoud Barzani was then succeeded by his nephew Nechirvan (BBC News 2019) (Hiltermann 2017). Furthermore, Iraqi Kurdistan is in a stalled transition, trapped in an obsolete order that fails to meet the expectations of a changing society. As a result, Iraqi Kurdistan's role as the hub for the evolution of Kurdish nationalism is declining (Salih and Fantappie 2019).

The Kurds and Iraq: Conclusion

Iraqi Kurds have experienced major discrimination and suppression by the Iraqi government. There is nothing worse in Kurdish history than the genocide of hundreds of thousands of Kurds during the regime of Saddam Hussein. Ultimately, the no-fly zone established by the US and its allies led to Iraqi Kurds gaining autonomy. KRG leader's attempted to capitalize on Iraq's weakness after forcing the Islamic State out of the region, but the independent referendum ultimately backfired. Though tensions following the referendum have subsided, it has yet to be seen how the KRG and the Kurds in general will proceed. Though it backfired, the independence referendum showed the world one fact: nearly every Kurd wants an independence Kurdish state. How that could be achieved, is yet to be seen. There is a difference 45 between what one wants to achieve, what is achievable, and what can be achieved ("Bakir: Kurdistan as a Model for Iraq" 2007).

CHAPTER 3

The Road to Sovereignty

Introduction

In this chapter, I highlight three key roadblocks for Kurdish statehood: lack of territory, the population's relationship with the state, and government institutions. I also highlight three internal issues that the Kurds have that are potential roadblocks to their own sovereignty and independence, as well as issues should they achieve statehood. These include: the Kurdish diaspora and returning populations, economic issues, especially oil, and the Kurd's own political divisions. These divisions are the biggest obstacle to creating a Kurdish state. The emergence of Kurdistan as a nation faces many internal and external factors.

State Building

The United Nations does not have a comprehensive agenda for state building. It is highly unlikely a framework would be successful in addressing the modern emergence of states, especially since they tend to emerge in post-conflict situations that are fractured. Each territory has its own unique and intricate political history and cultural disposition (Petrin 2002). The wide array of Kurdish political parties and groups reflects the internal divisions among Kurds, which often follow tribal, linguistic, and national fault lines, in addition to political disagreements and rivalries ("The Time of the Kurds" 2017).

Definition of a State

A state is defined as a territorial body with secure borders, a population, and a government that maintains sovereignty over its own territory and is recognized as sovereign by other states (Goldstein and Pevehouse 2018). It is a political entity with a recognized territory and a population that sees itself as belonging to the state, and institutions of governance that are sovereign within that state (Goodson 2001). With the definitions of a state in mind, the 47 following are three basic elements of an emergent state and potential roadblocks that must be addressed, solidified, and present for an independent Kurdish state to be established. The three specific problem areas that apply to Kurdistan are the lack of territory, the population's relationship with the state, and government institutions.

Territory

The territory and land itself of emergent states tend to be in dispute. This is not new or unique to Kurdistan. We see this with Israel and Palestine and the former Yugoslavia, specifically Kosovo and Bosnia (Petrin 2002). Border conflicts and disputes exist in every emergence of a state. The region of Kurdistan and the territory the Kurds claim as their homeland has been disputed for over one hundred years. Even amongst current Kurdish political leaders there is a dispute as to what land they lay claim to. This means Kurdistan has both internal and external territorial disputes. Before the state can be established the borders must be solidified and secured to some degree for the emergent state to stand a chance. If the territory remains in flux and contested territories and borders cannot be resolved, the state will remain instable, there will be a void in power and functionality and will result in a failed state (Petrin 2002).

Borders and territory are the first and most difficult external roadblock to Kurdish sovereignty and independence. The Kurds claim areas that are recognized to be the territory of already established, functioning and recognized states. Therefore, these states would have to cede territory to make way for Kurdistan to become a sovereign state. Iraq and Turkey would be unlikely to cede territory to the Kurds, though Kurds make up about 20% of the population of each state respectively ("Factbox: The Kurdish Struggle for Rights and Land—Reuters" 2019).

Iraq specifically has granted the Kurds autonomy in the Kurdistan Region of Iraq, but they still do not have sovereignty despite the overwhelming referendum vote in favor of independence.

The Population's Relationship with the State

The second basic element of an emergent state is the population's relationship with the state. In any emergent or existing state, a population's relationship with the state changes after conflict. In a time of war, the population may become focused on identities that render allegiance to their religion or ethnicity more significant than their nationality, such as in Afghanistan, where one's tribe became the primary focus of social and political organization in state absence. Forced displacement and exile can also have the opposite effect on a population, inspiring a kind of ultra-nationalism in which one's identity with the country of origin becomes the primary focus of social and political organization, as in the case of Rwandan Hutu refugees in Tanzania (Petrin 2002). Kurds generally fall into the latter category, but in the last decade, Kurdish nationalism has been faltering. Specifically, Iraqi Kurdistan's role as the center for the evolution of Kurdish nationalism is declining. Expectations and hopes had risen after the 2003 U.S. invasion of Iraq, especially among the younger generation, whom saw only the end of Saddam Hussein's regime and remember little of it. Many Kurds were even more exacerbated by the failed referendum (Salih and Fantappie 2019).

Government Institutions

Thirdly, in state building, government institutions and infrastructure tend to be weak or completely destroyed due to the fact emergent states usually involve and emerge out of interstate and/or intrastate conflict. These institutions and infrastructure may include, but is not limited to, roads, schools, hospitals, and bridges. The state may be barely capable of functioning and in this 49 weakened state transition becomes difficult. All of these factors affect Kurdistan's potential of statehood (Petrin 2002).

The Kurds have been considered second-class citizens in their homelands for centuries. Other than in Iraqi Kurdistan, they had no right to speak their own language or to wear traditional attire in state institutions. This now has an effect on infrastructure, education, and general state building. Due to the KRG's instability, students often pursue education in the surrounding nations. However, students must undergo security screening and Kurds are often excluded from some subjects, including electronics and aerospace engineering. After Saddam Hussein's reign and the war, the damaged infrastructure of Iraq's and Iran's Kurdish regions, often there was electricity for just a few hours each day, preventing research laboratories from functioning (Karimi 2020).

The Kurdistan Region of Iraq has produced major growth in infrastructure and construction since gaining autonomy, primarily the Irbil International Airport, roads, bridges, and public buildings ("Bakir: Kurdistan as a Model for Iraq" 2007). However, the region has suffered from several natural disasters, such as floods, made even worse by the lack of functioning infrastructure in the region and exacerbating efforts to improve. In addition, hundreds of infrastructure projects were put on hold for years because of the war against the Islamic State. The chaos and conflict the war caused a financial crisis, falling oil prices, refugee crisis, and budget cuts and disputes with Iraqi government. This halted further progress and further damaged an already fragile infrastructure. During the war, over two thousand infrastructure initiatives were stopped because of budget and financial constraints, according to Erbil governor Nawzad Hadi. Near the end of 2019, The Kurdistan Regional Government (KRG) 50 announced plans for regional infrastructure investment, specifically but not limited to transportation and services (Johnson 2019).

It is debatable whether or not the Kurdistan Region of Iraq could function and sustain itself independently, though many would argue with oil money it could. Either way, it is of the upmost importance that the KRG develop more housing, tourism, agricultural, and construction sectors. A strong economic foundation will be necessary for Kurdistan's future and possible independence. Iraqi Kurdistan largely escaped the privations of the last years of Saddam's rule and the chaos that followed his ouster in 2003 and built a parliamentary democracy with a growing economy. Major problems remain, nonetheless. The landlocked Kurdistan Region is surrounded by countries unsympathetic to Kurdish aspirations—namely Turkey, Syria and Iran (BBC News 2018).

Internal Roadblocks

The immediate tasks facing the Kurdish government have been numerous and intricate. These initial tasks have included rebuilding infrastructure, creating an administration and absorbing hundreds of thousands of displaced people after years of war and destruction. They have begun this process, but it is ongoing. Overall its efforts exceeded all expectations (BBC News 2018). As the victims of countless wars, betrayals, and suppression, it is easy to see the Kurd's struggle as all external. However, there are many existing issues that could either hinder the Kurds gaining independence or cripple them if not addressed. These internal potential roadblocks include: the Kurdish diaspora and returning populations, economic issues, especially oil, and the Kurd's own political divisions.

Kurdish Diaspora

Diasporas have a significant impact in ongoing social processes, either via remittances, investment, skills transfer, diaspora philanthropy or political influence (Başer 2019). A diaspora is inevitable without a national state for such a large people group. Not only have the Kurd's been stateless for all of their history, but genocide, international and civil wars, and Saddam Hussein, increased the long Kurdish diaspora. One hundred years of conflict has contributed to the diaspora of the Kurdish people. Furthermore, the Kurdish diaspora has led to a lack of unity within the diverse ethnicity, including culture, language, religion, and politics, leading to further conflict and division. Today, the geopolitical situation in Kurdistan is rapidly shifting. Kurds are flocking back home to Kurdistan, specifically the Kurdistan Regional Government of Iraq. What the Kurdish people and the region overall is experiencing is commonly referred to as a diasporic homecoming. There Kurds, upon returning home, want to aid and contribute to the development of Kurdistan, specifically the Kurdistan Region of Iraq (Başer and Toivanen 2019).

Kurdish Returning

The return of refugees is an integral aspect of state reconstruction that both offers substantial benefits and poses significant challenges to the state. Returnees lend a measure of internal legitimacy to the state, giving it international recognition and furnishing it with additional human resources for development. The manner in which emerging states respond to returnee needs in the post-conflict period serves as an indicator as to whether the state can meet its immediate development goals. Repatriation can be planned and managed in such a way that return contributes to strengthening national infrastructure, reconciliation efforts between opposing ethnic groups, and the renewal of conducive civil-state relations. When large-scale returns are unmanageable or poorly planned, internal displacement and urban bias pose significant challenges to emerging state infrastructure. The restoration of the state-citizen 52 relationship in the post-conflict period demands both a functional state and active civil society, both of which take years to develop and may be absent in certain contexts As far as why Kurds are returning back to their historical homeland, there is no single reason. One study found that some Kurds have returned because of failure to integrate in the host country while others have had more altruistic or financial motives in their decision to return (Başer 2019). Diasporas inevitably cause brain drain: the departure of educated or professional people from one country, economic sector, or field for another usually for better pay or living conditions ("Brain Drain | Definition of Brain Drain by Merriam-Webster" n.d.). The Kurdish diaspora is no exception. Now, on returning it is not that diasporans lack the will or capacity to transfer knowledge, but rather that they lack the structure and strategy to do so and the Kurdistan Region of Iraq has, so far, failed to implement a program or structure to engage returning diasporans and allow them to contribute. The Kurdistan Regional Government has made promises to collaborate and include diasporans, but there are

currently no policies in place or being created to institution-
alize or administer such things (Başer 2019).

Setting up a central body in charge of developing ministries and departments is vital in state reconstruction and
building. Managing the return and meeting returnee's basic
needs and aiding in reintegration often become the first
national objective of a transitional state. However, the KRG
has failed to prioritize this. Preparing for repatriation facili-
tates the process of building government institutions; priori-
tizing returnee integration could aid in further infrastructure
development (Petrin 2002).

Considering the current crisis that the KRG has been
facing since 2013, it is possible to argue that contributions
of those returning after the diaspora matter more than ever,
as other types of foreign direct investment will likely decline.
However, the opportunities that the KRG 53 can offer to
the diasporans and returnees have also been affected by these
recent developments and lack of infrastructure. The KRG
could not pay the salaries of civil servants for a long time,
the unemployment rate is strikingly high and the KRG still
does not offer diaspora-specific incentives for economic
investments. The post referendum developments failed to
trigger diasporic patriotism. If anything, the referendum
hurt the population's relationship with the state more than it
improved it. Furthermore, returnees complain about corruption, nepotism and rivalries among Kurdish political parties
as the biggest problems that the KRG must address in the
future. There is a risk that these problems could trigger a
re-return to the host countries (Baser & Toivanen, 2018).
It has been reported that many young Kurds have started
to leave Kurdistan during the last five years (Başer 2019)
(Eccarius-Kelly, 2018). In conclusion, recent developments
show that the KRG desperately requires a more systematic

and sustainable diaspora engagement strategy to revitalize diaspora-homeland relations and create more opportunities for cooperation.

Economic Roadblocks to Independence

Given the Kurds' long history of persecution and deep desire for a state, many wonder why they haven't just declared independence from Iraq already. There are a number of reasons, including American opposition and that Kurdistan is dependent on payments from the Iraqi central government, but a big one is oil, which is the Kurd's primary route to financial independence. However, they don't yet produce enough to be economically self-sufficient and they don't have legal authority to sell it directly on the market. Furthermore, the Kurds lack the infrastructure to export enough oil to make independence financially advantageous (Beauchamp 2014).

Under the current arrangement, the Baghdad government is supposed to handle Kurdish oil sales. They then take the proceeds and divvy them up among the different regions. Kurdistan is supposed to get 17 percent of the nation's oil sales, but Kurdish leaders say they're given less than that. So, they've tested out the waters on selling oil directly, largely to Turkey, in early 2014, but Baghdad retaliated, and started cutting off federal funding and oil payments to the Kurdish government from the oil-sharing agreement so the KRG reagreed to the previous arrangement because the Kurds survive on that oil money, furthering their dependency on Baghdad (Beauchamp 2014).

The economic case against secession rests largely on oil. Since gaining de facto autonomy in the early 1990s under a U.S.-imposed no-fly zone, Iraqi Kurds have steadily built up institutions including ministries, a civil service, and an army, allowing them to effectively function as a state. They have had less success developing economic self-reliance, however, largely because steady petroleum revenues have stifled the incentive to diversify into other sectors, like agriculture, manufacturing, and banking—as well as developing their capacity to collect taxes. Instead, the Kurdistan Regional Government relies on oil sales for up to 90 percent of its revenues, which, in turn, are spent overwhelmingly on the salaries of government employees who underpin the region's workforce. As with other rentier economies, those dependent on external monies and profit, private-sector activity such as construction depends heavily on public spending (Dziadosz 2017).

The KRG produces roughly 600,000 barrels of oil per day. These are almost exclusively piped through Turkey to the port of Ceyhan. Therefore, Ankara has enormous leverage over the KRG's economy though the resource-distribution systems underlying social and economic stability. Geographically, the KRG is landlocked and therefore dependent on surrounding states 55 allowing them to export through their ports. The KRG's economy depends on one pipeline that goes through Turkey and sells oil to international markets. If that pipeline was shut down or the KRG was barred from using that pipeline, the Kurdish economy would cease to function completely. The other major problem is the region's heavy reliance on imports, which account for some 80 to 90 percent of goods, analysts estimate. The region produces significant amounts of cement, steel, and wheat, but little else. Again, because Kurdistan is land-locked, closing its borders with Iran or Turkey or airspace through Iraq would swiftly lead to sharp spikes in prices or shortages of basic goods such as food and fuel. A coordinated blockade by the region's neighbors would be devastating (Dziadosz 2017).

But Kurdistan doesn't have to rely solely on oil. Its fertile farmland and central location could make it a hub for regional trade; focusing more attention on other internal revenues could soften the blow of any blockade by neighboring countries in the future. As to why the KRG has failed to exploit or began developing these other avenues, most analysts point to corruption. Building party loyalty has dictated the logic of much of the region's development, with sectors that are difficult to tie into patronage networks, such as agriculture, flagging from neglect, while those which more easily facilitate kickbacks, such as construction, have boomed (Dziadosz 2017). If future strides are not taken economically, any attempts toward statehood and independence will prove futile. Without economic self-sufficiency, Kurdish independence will always stand on shaky ground.

Political Division

Compared to the rest of Iraq, Kurdistan enjoys more stability, security, political pluralism, and freedom for civil society. From 2003 until 2013, the region witnessed an unprecedented economic boom. During the U.S.-led war to depose Saddam Hussein, the Kurds 56 were some of the United States' most reliable allies and they played a pivotal role in the fight against the Islamic State. But today, this nascent democracy faces its most severe and probably decisive crisis since the end of its civil war in 1998, which had pitted the region's two main political camps against each other. Today's crisis touches upon two core democratic principles: the peaceful transfer of power and government accountability (Hassan 2015). The Kurds' disunity is cited by experts as one of the primary causes for their inability to form a state of their own.

Political division, in particular, a rivalry between the main parties, has proved to be a major impediment to the political development and stability of the KRG (Abdullah 2018). The Kurdistan Region of Iraq's government is technically a multi-party system. In a multi-party system, several dozen political parties participate in elections, this is the governmental system of countries like Germany or France. In reality though, only two parties in the Kurdistan Region of Iraq's government hold any influence. The two parties, The Kurdistan Democratic Party (KDP) and the Patriotic Union of Kurdistan (PUK), have existed since before the Kurdistan Region of Iraq.

The two parties have been in conflict since the mid-1970's, ranging from times of tension to times of outright violence. In the 1990s, it degenerated into open warfare between armed groups loyal to each party. It got to the point where, in 1996, the KDP asked for Saddam's help in rooting the PUK out of Erbil, which it controlled (Beauchamp 2014). It wasn't until post Saddam Hussein that the region experienced political organization in the Kurdistan Region Government. Though the two parties have formed a sort of tactical alliance and they cooperate, the Kurds still remain divided. Moreover, it wasn't until this last decade other parties have emerged, though they have yet to gain much control in the region. Some of these emerging 57 parties include New Generation, the Coalition for Democracy and Justice, and several Islamic parties. Current trends and data slight growth of outside parties besides the two dominating ones, the PUK and KDP, though they still retain the power (Abdullah 2018).

What is interesting is that there doesn't appear to be much of an ideological disagreement between the two parties. The PUK itself came in practice and behavior to resemble the KDP so much that the average Kurds were often unable to specify a single policy or ideological disagreement between the two (Beauchamp 2014). The main controversy between the KDP and the PUK is over what type of system the government of the KRG should have, a parliamentary or a presidential system. The PUK wants to establish a parliamentary system while the KDP desires to establish a presidential system. These two parties both want to implement their desired system and agenda upon the region and by proxy are the two driving forces of KRI's political instability (Abdullah 2018).

The Failed Referendum

Some experts argue the referendum and the autonomous Kurdistan Region of Iraq overall has been a failed attempt to establish a stable political system and thus a failure to establish a sovereign state. Though various common trademarks of political authority are present in the KRG, it has still been unable to create a unified political system in the past few decades (Abdullah 2018). Furthermore, the referendum not only failed to achieve independence, but also backfired by drawing international ire and provoking Baghdad to reinstate its authority in disputed territories and Iraqi Kurdistan's airspace (Salih and Fantappie 2019).

While Barzani felt that the time was ripe to press for secession from Iraq, coming just as the Islamic State was being pushed from its last holdouts in the country's north, the state of Kurdistan's economy suggests just the opposite. With a near-complete dependency on imports 58 for basic goods and on oil piped through Turkey for government revenues, Kurdish leaders had no leverage in post-referendum negotiations. Furthermore, as it stands now, an independent Kurdistan's economy would not be viable (Dziadosz 2017).

Conclusion

The road to an independent Kurdistan is a long and complicated one with no end nearing. In conclusion, there are both external and internal factors that affect the would-be emergent state of Kurdistan. In order to successfully secede and achieve independence, Kurdistan will first have to secure territory and borders and have a more functioning government and infrastructure. However, the KRG's poor handling of the diasporic returning populations, economic instability, especially oil reliance, will likely be much more detrimental to their own attempts at independence than any other external issues or forces. Furthermore, the most damaging of them all being the Kurd's own political division. Though common ethnic identity may unite them, as a people, they are still as divided as any other ethnic group—by dialect, political ideology, and the personalities and strategic priorities of their leaders (Hiltermann 2017). If the Kurds hope to establish an independent Kurdistan they must engage diasporic-returnees, stabilize and build their infrastructure, build a more sustainable economic plan, and seek political unity and functioning democracy.

CONCLUSION

The purpose of this paper is to give a starting place of historical context and background in order to holistically assess and understand the Kurd's current status and identify areas of weakness in their fight for sovereignty and independence. Though Kurds have achieved autonomy in Iraq, they still face external and internal roadblocks to sovereignty. Further research revealed that internal issues perhaps pose more of a roadblock than external ones, specifically, economic and political instability and division being the most problematic.

Research revealed that in a historical context, the years of war and suppression furthered the Kurdish diaspora and has prevented the Kurds from achieving independence. They were cut out of a state in the split of the Ottoman Empire and have been denied ever since. Not only do regional powers currently oppose the formation of a Kurdish state, but they have actively suppressed the Kurd's basic rights and engaged in violent disputes historically. The worst of it culminated in the genocidal campaign launched by Saddam Hussein against Iraqi Kurds. However, the downfall of Hussein and the establishment of the no-fly zone enabled the Kurds to gain de facto autonomy in the region and eventually establish the Kurdistan Regional Government of Iraq. Yet, they are still seeking the establishment of an independent Kurdish state.

The emergence of new states often is met with some amount of skepticism, especially by neighboring states already in existence. The Kurds are no exception. There are many factors as to why surrounding states and the United States do not support the Kurd's quest for a state of their own: fear of armed conflicts, regional instability, surging nationalism, or simply out of complacency and desire to leave things as they are. However, emergent states can offer many possibilities for sustainable development, Kurdistan is no exception (Gudrich 2016). However, 60 rather than being defined by the international community, transitional states, in this instance Kurdistan, should be given the opportunity to redefine itself within their given context. Though the international community can effectively support the reconstruction Kurdistan in the post conflict period, the ultimate process of state regeneration is a long-term process that rests with the state and its people (Petrin 2002).

Research suggest that the best next step for the Kurds in their fight to attain a sovereignty state, is not in gaining territory but focusing on strengthening the KRG's economy, democracy, and infrastructure. Their reliance on Iraq and Turkey for funding and support has and will keep them crippled and prevent them from gaining independence. Any attempts to gain independence have and will continue to fail if they cannot strengthen their existing regions so they can be sustainable in the eventual independent Kurdish state. In this study, further research on key reasons fueling the KRG's political instability and corruption would help further theorize on policies and action steps. A study on young Kurds, those returning to the region and those leaving could also hold answers and help likely projection as to what the future may hold for the Kurds. Furthermore, it would be helpful to begin research on what it would take to get the surrounding states to negotiate for an independent Kurdish state and how they could make that transition peacefully.

WORK CITED

Abdullah, Farhad Hassan. 2018. "The Political System in Iraqi Kurdistan: Party Rivalries and Future Perspectives." Asian Affairs 49 (4): 606–24. https://doi.org/ 10.1080/0306837 4.2018.1521120.

"Bakir: Kurdistan as a Model for Iraq." 2007. Council on Foreign Relations. Accessed August 23, 2020. https://www. cfr.org/interview/bakir-kurdistan-model-iraq.

Başer, Bahar. 2019. "Engaging Diasporas in Development and State-Building: The Role of the Kurdish Diaspora and Returnees in Rebuilding the Kurdistan Region of Iraq." Ethnopolitics 18 (1): 76–91. https://doi.org/10.1080/1744 9057.2018.1525167.

Başer, Bahar, and Mari Toivanen. 2019. "Diasporic Homecomings to the Kurdistan Region of Iraq: Pre- and Post-Return Experiences Shaping Motivations to Re-Return." Ethnicities 19 (5): 901–24. https://doi. org/10.1177/1468796818757265.

BBC News. 2014. "Turkey's Fear of a Reignited Kurdish Flame," October 8, 2014, sec. Europe. https://www.bbc.com/news/world-middle-east-29542040.

BBC News. 2016. "Who Are Kurdistan Workers' Party (PKK) Rebels?," November 4, 2016, sec. Europe. https://www.bbc.com/news/world-europe-20971100.

BBC News. 2017. "Iraqi Kurdistan Profile—Timeline," October 31, 2017, sec. Middle East. https://www.bbc.com/news/world-middle-east-15467672.

BBC News. 2018. "Iraqi Kurdistan Profile," April 25, 2018, sec. Middle East. https://www.bbc.com/news/world-middle-east-28147263.

BBC News. 2019. "Who Are the Kurds?," October 15, 2019, sec. Middle East. https://www.bbc.com/news/world-middle-east-29702440.

Beauchamp, Zack. 2014. "6 Essential Facts about Iraq's Kurds." Vox. August 12, 2014. 62 https://www.vox.com/2014/8/12/5991425/kurds-iraq-kurdistan-peshmerga.

"Brain Drain | Definition of Brain Drain by Merriam-Webster." n.d. Accessed September 29, 2020. https://www.merriam-webster.com/dictionary/brain%20drain. Bruno, Greg. 2007. "Inside the Kurdistan Workers Party (PKK)."

Council on Foreign Relations. 2007. https://www.cfr.org/backgrounder/inside-kurdistan-workers-party-pkk. Chmaytelli, Raya Jalabi, Maher. 2017.

"Kurdish Leader Barzani Resigns after Independence Vote Backfires." Reuters, October 30, 2017. https://www.reuters.com/article/us-mideastcrisis-iraq-kurds-barzani-idUSKBN1CY0KR.

Danforth, Nick. 2015. "Forget Sykes-Picot. It's the Treaty of Sèvres That Explains the Modern Middle East." Foreign Policy. 2015.

https://foreignpolicy.com/2015/08/10/sykes-picottreaty-of-sevres-modern-turkey-middle-east-borders-turkey/.

Dziadosz, Alex. 2017. "The Economic Case Against an Independent Kurdistan." The Atlantic.

September 26, 2017. https://www.theatlantic.com/international/archive/2017/09/

kurdistan-barzani-iraq-turkey-blockade-oil/541149/.

"Factbox: The Kurdish Struggle for Rights and Land." 2019. Reuters. 2019. https://www.reuters.com/article/us-syria-security-kurds-factbox/factbox-the-kurdishstruggle-for-rights-and-land-idUSKBN1WO19X.

Goldstein, Joshua S, and Jon C. Pevehouse. 2018. International Relations. 11th edition. Pearson.

Goodson, Larry P. 2001. Afghanistan's Endless War: State Failure, Regional Politics and the Rise of the Taliban. London: University of Washington Press.

Gudrich, Nicholas. 2016. "GRIN—The Emergence of New States as a Chance for Sustainability

Politics. The Catalan Independence Movement." GRIN. 2016.

https://www.grin.com/document/337747. 63

Hassan, Kawa. 2015. "Kurdistan's Democracy on the Brink." Carnegie Middle East Center. 2015. https://carnegie-mec.org/2015/10/28/kurdistan-s-democracy-on-brink-pub-61810.

Hasan, Harith. 2019. "Boundary Disputes." Carnegie Middle East Center. September 26, 2019.

https://carnegie-mec.org/diwan/79875.

Hiltermann, Joost. 2017. "The Kurds Are Right Back Where They Started." Crisis Group.

October 31, 2017. https://www.crisisgroup.org/middle-east-north-africa/gulf-and-arabianpeninsula/iraq/kurds-are-right-back-where-they-started.

"History | Unbelievable Kurdistan—Official Tourism Site of Kurdistan." n.d. Accessed August 22, 2020. http://bot.gov.krd/about-kurdistan/history.

Johnson, Holly. 2019. "KRG Announces $420mn in Infrastructure Spending." Rudaw. 2019. https://www.rudaw.net/english/kurdistan/171020191. Karimi, Ebrahim. 2020.

"Kurdistan: Instability Wrecks Research and Education." Nature 577 (7790): 318–318. https://doi.org/10.1038/d41586-020-00057-w.

"Kurdistan | History, Religion, & Facts." n.d. Encyclopedia Britannica. Accessed October 2, 2020. https://www.britannica.com/place/Kurdistan.

"Land & Environment." n.d. Official Site of General Board of Tourism of Kurdistan—Iraq.

Accessed October 2, 2020. http://bot.gov.krd/about-kurdistan/land-environment.

"Learn About Kurdish Culture." n.d. The Kurdish Project (blog). Accessed October 24, 2020.

https://thekurdishproject.org/history-and-culture/kurdish-culture/.

"Learn About Kurdish Language." n.d. The Kurdish Project (blog). Accessed October 23, 2020.

https://thekurdishproject.org/history-and-culture/kurdish-culture/kurdish-language/.

MacDonald, Alex. 2019. "'No Friends but the Mountains': History Repeats Itself with Latest US 64

Betrayal of Kurds." Middle East Eye. 2019. http://www.middleeasteye.net/news/kurdshistory-betrayal.

Petrin, Sarah Dawn. 2002. "Refugee Return and State Reconstruction: A Comparative Analysis."

United Nations High Commissioner for Refugees, Evaluation and Policy Analysis Unit

(Working Paper No. 66): 25.

Pitel, Laura, and Chloe Cornish. 2019. "A 100-Year Struggle: The Kurdish Fight for Land and Identity." https://www.ft.com/content/871c10c2-e9c3-11e9-85f4-d00e5018f061.

Salih, Cale, and Maria Fantappie. 2019. "Kurdish Nationalism at an Impasse." The Century

Foundation. April 29, 2019. https://tcf.org/content/report/iraqi-kurdistan-losing-placecenter-kurdayeti/.

Tabatabai, Ariane M. 2017. "Iran and the Kurds," November 29, 2017. https://www.foreignaffairs.com/articles/iran/2017-09-26/iran-and-kurds.

"The Time of the Kurds." 2017. Council on Foreign Relations. 2017. https://on.cfr.org/1Q9PWRG.

"Timeline: The Kurds' Quest for Independence." n.d. Council on Foreign Relations. Accessed

August 23, 2020. https://www.cfr.org/timeline/kurds-quest-independence.

Zanotti, Jim, and Clayton Thomas. 2019. "The Kurds in Iraq, Turkey, Syria, and Iran."

Congressional Research Service.

WORLDVIEW APPENDIX

My Christian worldview calls me to believe in justice and to fight injustice. I think anyone reading on the Kurds would agree they have been wronged and my faith calls me to fight for their justice as if it were my own. Though the Kurds are primarily of different religion, they are considered moderates in the region and have been key to fighting Islamic extremists. It is this fact that largely contributed to the United States decisions to support the Kurds in various wars and battles. Though they have different belief than I do, I celebrate religious freedom and what they fight for. However, it has commonly been said, "one country's freedom fighter, is another country's terrorist." My faith does not promote violence so though I do support an independent Kurdistan, there are many instances I have morally disagreed with the choices of some groups of Kurds, specifically militant groups that believe in unprovoked violence.

However, this is in tension as my faith also calls me to have compassion for them. So, though I do not condone violence, I am filled with compassion for the Kurds and sympathetic to their plight and can do so without agree with their every action.

This topic interests with a Christian worldview as are called to bring hope, peace, and justice to the world. This may look many different ways, but I believe we can bring hope and support to Kurdistan even if just through prayers and financial support through non-profits and local charities. I believe we are called to pursue justice and promote peace as Christians, and I believe Kurdistan is key to peace in the region.

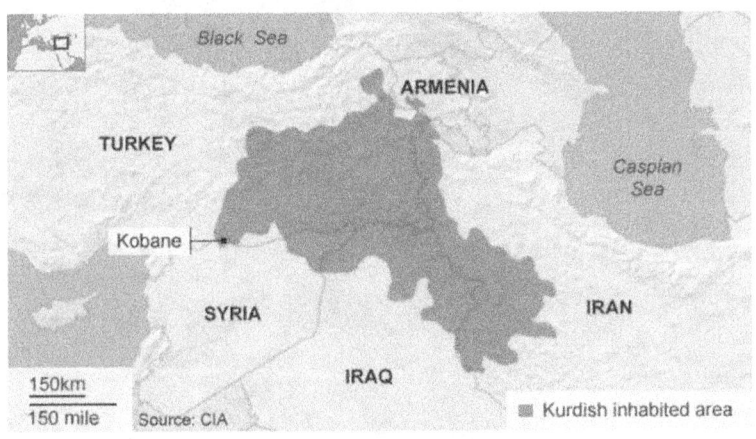

30 MILLION KURDS

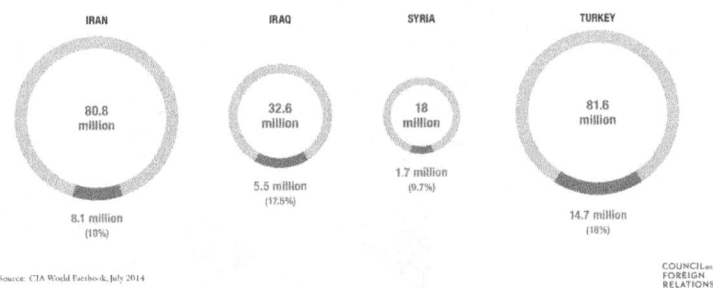

Source: CIA World Factbook, July 2014

CPSIA information can be obtained
at www.ICGtesting.com
Printed in the USA
BVHW071106030621
608731BV00003B/561